Beware the Straw Man
The Science Dog Explores Dog Training Fact & Fiction

Linda P. Case

Beware the Straw Man
The Science Dog Explores Dog Training Fact & Fiction
Linda P. Case

AutumnGold Publishing
A Division of AutumnGold Consulting
Mahomet, IL 61853
www.autumngoldconsulting.com

ISBN-13: 978-1495389771
ISBN-10: 1495389774

Other Books by Linda P. Case

Dog Food Logic: Making Smart Decisions for your Dog in an Age of Too Many Choices

Canine and Feline Behavior and Training: A Complete Guide to Understanding our Two Best Friends

Canine and Feline Nutrition: A Resource for Companion Animal Professionals

The Dog: Its Behavior, Nutrition and Health

The Cat: Its Behavior, Nutrition and Health

To Cadie

Table of Contents

Introduction

If you are reading this book, I am pretty certain that you live with one or more dogs, have friends and possibly family who love dogs, enjoy dog-related activities or sports, and if you are lucky, may even be able to count a dog-related profession or volunteer effort as part of your life. In other words, like me, you proudly identify yourself as a "*dog person*".

Like some of you, I have been lucky enough during my life to have had the opportunity to combine my passion for "all things dog" with my professional life. For me that has meant working as a university lecturer, writer and dog trainer. I left academia a few years ago to concentrate more on writing about dogs. This book is one of the products of that life change. Currently, my husband Mike and I live with our four dogs; Cadie, Vinny, Chip and Cooper, plus, Pete the cat (who likes dogs well enough but does wonder why anyone would be interested enough to write about them).

So, why a book about dogs and science? Why not just about dogs? The answer to this has to do with the decisions that we make for our dogs. As their caretakers and advocates, we make many decisions for our dogs each and every day. Some of these judgments are simple and mundane – *Shall we walk in the park this morning or stroll through the neighborhood? Do you want to play with your blue ball or your yellow stuffed tiger? No, I have decided that you cannot chase Pete the cat (he really does not like it, despite what you think).* In contrast, other decisions that we make for our dogs have greater importance with respect to their safety and life quality. *Should I use training methods that emphasize rewards or that focus on punishment? Is turning my back when you jump up an effective training technique? Is there a way in which I can predict if you are going to be aggressive to children or guard your food bowl? Is it true that you will be a hyperactive and bratty dog simply because you are small?* For these more important decisions, we have science and the evidence that it collects to guide us.

In *"Beware the Straw Man"*, we look at the scientific evidence that supports or refutes many commonly held beliefs about dog behavior and training. Each of the book's 32 essays identifies a common belief about dogs and then reviews the scientific evidence for and against that belief. Because each essay addresses a discrete topic, the format allows the reader to peruse the titles and select those topics that are of greatest interest. For example, if you are a budding citizen scientist and would like to learn more about the scientific method and how canine behavior studies are conducted by researchers, the *"Steve Series"* in Part 1 (Science) will be right for you. Other essays in this section examine a phenomenon that has been aptly labeled the "caregiver placebo effect" (*Consider the Placebo*), and provide ways to assess the reliability of information that you read or hear about dogs (*Thyroid on Trial*).

If you enjoy learning about recent advances in our understanding of canine behavior and cognition, Part 2 (Behavior) is where you might start. This section includes essays about the intricacies and uniqueness of the dog's special senses; the nose (*Smell This!*), hearing (*Its all Rock and Roll to Me*) and vocalizations (*You Barkin' at Me?*). For people who work with fearful or anxious dogs, *Fear Factor* and *Talking Turkey* in Part 2 and *Fear Itself* in Part 4 review new research about the effects of fear on dogs, our perceptions of those emotions, and possible ways of treating it. The final two essays in Part 2 are the most controversial; each critically reviews recent data from studies of standardized behavior tests that are used by animal shelters to assess dogs prior to adoption (*This Test You Keep Using* and *Beware the Straw Man*). Regardless of your current opinion about these tests, the information in these two essays should stimulate thought and discussion about their effectiveness and use.

Part 3 (Training) contains essays that explore the fundamental philosophies and tools of dog training. Many aspects of dog training are hotly debated, with people falling into various camps regarding what is best for dogs, what training approach is most effective, and how dogs learn most efficiently. Here we look at the science of operant and classical conditioning (*Deconstructing the Click*) and review studies that examine dogs' responses to different forms of reinforcement (*Treat, Please!*, *Speaking of Treats*, and *The Consequences of Consequences*). For instructors, we examine studies of a commonly used behavior modification method to reduce jumping (*Is it Time for the Extinction of Extinction?*) and the practice of handling students' dogs during a class (*Hey Teacher! Leave those Dogs Alone!*). Regardless of your current practices and beliefs about training, the information in this section will stimulate thought and discussion regarding what the current science is telling us about training methods and how dogs learn from and react to them.

We cannot examine dog behavior and training without including the individual at the other end of the lead – the human. The final section of "*Beware the Straw Man*" (Part 4 – Dogs & Their People) is a series of essays that examine how we live with, love, and treat the dogs in our lives. With each passing year, evidence continues to mount for the existence of emotions in dogs that were previously presumed to exist only in humans. The essays *I Yawn for Your Love* and *Lend a Helping Paw* review studies that further enlighten us about the dog's internal emotional life. It is also true that our relationships with dogs often influence our interactions with other people in our lives and in our communities. Two essays, *Love Me, Love My* Dog and *Dog Park People* take a closer look at these relationships and interactions. We all know that dogs can both be of great service to us and, in some situations, a potential threat to our safety. *The Sniff(th) Sense* and *The Kids are Alright* take us to both of ends of the spectrum of dog-human relationships.

Finally, in the book's attempt to stick to the scientific evidence ("*Just the Facts, Ma'am*"), one may ask if I, the author, ever venture to offer an opinion. Well, yes, as a matter of fact, I do. Sometimes, as you will see, it is just too difficult to refrain from including my personal view about topics that I have personal and professional experience with and that I may hold strong opinions about (remember, like you, I too am a dedicated dog person). On other occasions I may include an opinion as a way to challenge current thinking, stimulate discussion, and well, just to shake things up a bit. To alert the reader to those instances when I am straying from the dominion of science into the realm of opinion, the book includes this charming icon:

Up on my Soapbox

Not subtle, but it gets the message across. And of course, readers are welcome to read my opinions, to agree or not agree, and to find additional evidence in support or in dissent of the presented science. The ultimate goal of *"Beware the Straw Man"* is to encourage all who love dogs to seek out and critically review the evidence that science collects regarding beliefs and practices of dog care and training. Doing so will aid you in making informed and defendable decisions for your dog, to develop your own opinions, and if you like, to jump up upon your own soap box!

Part 1 - Science

1
Your Face Is Gonna Freeze Like That.....
(Observations)

Can dogs, like people, be emotionally primed? How would we study this question with our canine companions?

"You know, your face is going to freeze like that!" This common rebuke, uttered by moms everywhere, is typically directed toward crabby toddlers, sullen teens, and the occasional discontented failed-to-launch 29-year-old. We all know that the implied consequence of having one's face freeze like that is to remain perpetually in a bad mood; a mood that will plague us for the rest of our natural lives and that will make ourselves and everyone who has the misfortune of being in our presence utterly miserable. Generally, this is not something that one considers to be a good thing.

And of course, our moms are right. We should avoid getting into a habit of being in an unpleasant mood and expressing the sour face that goes along with it. That is the naturally accepted sequence of how things work: "*I feel unhappy, so I frown. I feel happy, so I smile*". And in many cases, this appears to be true. However, there is new research suggesting that this sequence can also be reversed. In other words, when we assume the physical trappings of happiness (smiling, laughter, high fives), we suddenly find ourselves *feeling* happier. Likewise, force your face into a frown, make the sour face that your mom chastised you about, or raise the finger that is interpreted as the polar opposite of *"have a good day"* and you will suddenly find yourself experiencing a less than sunny countenance.

When I first learned of this research and about what it implies for human behavior, I realized that this phenomenon might also impact certain methods that are used in dog training, and ultimately, the behavior of our dogs as well. In addition, this new information lends itself to a great example of *how science works* and how one might go about testing this hypothesis with actual dogs. Let's first look at the studies that were conducted with people and what they have shown to be true about human emotions.

In a nutshell, the studies suggest that the physical attributes of emotional states as well as emotionally-charged gestures can influence and can even cause the internal experience of the associated emotional state. In other words, while we traditionally have believed the sequence to be "I feel happy; therefore I smile", there is evidence showing that the opposite sequence of "I smile, then I feel happy" also applies and may even dominate in some circumstances. As a simple test, give this a try. Without intentionally thinking of something pleasant or pleasurable, move the muscles on your face into a smile. Wait 30 seconds, holding the smile. Now, how do you feel? How is your mood? Better? The same? Worse? When this was tested with groups of people, most reported that they felt happier after engaging in "smile behavior" even when the smile did not occur as a response to a pleasant event.

The Studies: Fritz Strack and Sabbine Stepper of Mannheim University and Leonard Martin of the University of Illinois examined the effects of physically inducing a smile or a frown in the absence of an attendant emotional event in a group of 92 undergraduate students (the usual subjects of many psychology experiments conducted in the University system) (1). The students were divided into three groups and each person was given a pencil to hold while completing a simple task. Group 1 was instructed to hold the pencil in their teeth, which naturally activates muscles used in smiling; Group 2 was instructed to hold the pencil pursed in their lips, which causes muscular changes associated with a frown, and Group 3 (the control group), held the pencil in their hand. These two pencil-holding techniques are quite effective at causing facial expressions associated with a either a smile or a frown. (It is important to keep in mind that the study participants had no hint that these facial manipulations were activated or that they caused smiles versus frowns).

Participants were then asked to read and rate a series of cartoons. The results? Those whose faces were forced into a smile rated the cartoons to be much funnier and more enjoyable than participants whose faces had been induced to frown. The researchers, along with those of several follow-up studies, concluded that even a contrived smile — one that is induced without an underlying emotional cause – has the effect of inducing a more positive (happy) emotional state in a person. In other words, if your face freezes in a smile, you will feel happier, and your mom was right - if your face freezes in a frown, you will feel perpetually unhappy. (Moms love this research).

There is more. These effects are not just associated with facial expressions, but can be manipulated with other, um, less socially acceptable expressions. Another group of researchers looked at how *hand gestures* might influence emotional states, again, when completely unrelated to events at hand (2). In a cleverly designed experiment, the investigators informed participants that they were studying the effects of arm movement upon reading ability. Similar to the smile study, participants were divided into three groups, each of which was asked to move their arm up and down repeatedly while reading a short essay. Each group was given specific instructions about how to hold their hand and move their arm, ostensibly to allow for proper measurements. Group 1 held their fist with a "thumbs-up" expression (positive emotion group); Group 2 held out their index finger (neutral emotion; control group); and Group 3 held out their middle finger (uh....the negative emotion group). If you are a bit confused, by the third group, consider the gesture that you are likely to see from the driver of a car that you unintentionally cut off in the middle of city traffic during a weekday rush-hour if you live in the United States. Got it?

The essay that everyone read described a man (George) who was refusing to pay his rent because his landlord had not made a set of promised repairs. After gesturing as they read, participants completed a questionnaire in which they rated George's behavior. Once again, contrived body gestures influenced an individual's emotions and perceptions. People in the "thumbs-up" group rated George significantly more favorably than did people in the neutral group or than people in the negative emotion group. In fact the people who were "flippin' the bird" while reading rated George very critically.

In other words, their perceptions of the same individual in the same circumstances were influenced by manipulating seemingly unrelated, but emotionally-charged gestures. Manipulations that were associated with positive social emotions ("thumbs up"; way to go!) appeared to put people in a generous and friendly state of mind (*George is a good guy; he was forced to behave badly by a difficult situation*). Conversely, causing people to make a gesture that is associated with very negative social emotions and that generally does not lead to good feelings, caused people to be more judgmental and critical of another (*What a slacker and low-life that George is; he should have paid his rent like a responsible adult*). Most amazing? The folks in each group were completely unaware that their emotional states had been influenced prior to voicing their opinions of George.

So, what does any of this have to do with dogs or dog training? After all, these are studies with human subjects, not with dogs. True. However, we regularly influence and manipulate dogs both physically and emotionally when we train them and modify their behaviors. (Actually, that is what training is). So, can we use science to determine if this information is applicable to dogs?

CITED STUDIES:

1. Strack F, Martin LL, Stepper S. Inhibiting and facilitating conditions of the human smile: a nonobtrusive test of the facial feedback hypothesis. *Journal of Perspectives of Society* 1988; 54:768-777.

2. Chandler J, Schwarz N. How extending your middle finger affects your perception of others: Learned movements influence concept accessibility, *Journal of Experimental Social Psychology* 2009; 45:123-128.

2
Your Face is Gonna Freeze Like That.....
(The Hypothesis)

Can "touch-then-treat" be improved with priming?

As we have seen, there is evidence suggesting that human emotional states can (rather easily it appears) be manipulated, and that this manipulation influences our perceptions and opinions of unrelated events. When your face is forced into a smile, you feel happy; likewise when it is forced into a frown, your mood darkens. Similar results occur with socially acceptable and no-so-acceptable hand gestures. Let us now turn to how this new information might be applicable to dog training and how we could set up a hypothesis to test its existence.

Most dog trainers and owners are intimately aware of and concerned with the emotional states of their dogs. The goal of many dog trainers, including myself, is to use training methods that promote relaxation, comfort, and general feelings of happiness in dogs, as we teach them desired behaviors. The use of clicker training and behavior modification programs that use classically-conditioned pleasurable responses are two examples of this philosophy in action.

Touch-Then-Treat: One application of classical conditioning that can be used to build pleasant associations between stimuli is the "touch-then-treat" method. I use this regularly in my own training school to teach young dogs that various types of handling (touching) reliably predict something pleasurable (a treat). The application of "touch-then-treat" is simple - owners first touch (handle a paw, look in an ear, gently restrain) then immediately treat (yummy goodie, pleasant voice). If practiced consistently, various types of handling (touch) come to reliably predict something pleasant (a treat) *rather than something unpleasant* (putting medications in ears, clipping nails, restraint for injections). This is an important concept as well as an easy and fun training technique. We use it because it is very easy to get into a habit of only handling our dogs' ears, feet, mouths when we need to clean ears, wipe off feet or brush teeth. Even worse, handling may only be initiated when there is a problem or health condition – for example, to remove a tick from an ear or to administer pills.

Think of it like this. Reaching out and grabbing your dog's ear and looking inside is not a behavior that we as owners are inclined to do spontaneously. In fact, I would venture that most of us, in the absence of considering a touch-treat protocol, do not regularly handle our dog's ears in a way that is similar to the actions that we use to clean the ear canal or administer medications. Similarly, how often do you impulsively pick up your dog's paws, examine them, and put them down again *without* cutting nails or wiping feet? His mouth? Same scenario. It is simply the normal state of affairs that reaching for an ear, picking up a foot and restraining our dog's head to open up his mouth become predictors for our dog that *"something icky is about to happen"* We unintentionally set our dogs up for reacting with fear or avoidance (or even nervous aggression) if we neglect to ensure that the vast majority of handling experiences predict good things happening rather than painful or uncomfortable things. The intent of touch-then-treat exercises is to shift the balance in favor of pleasant associations and away from unpleasant associations. If a dog finds that the vast majority of "touch experiences" lead to a tasty treat rather than an unpleasant pill, the risk that he will begin to avoid being handled is greatly reduced. The ultimate goal is a dog who has a pleasurable emotional response (and so behaves calmly) to most types of handling rather than an unpleasant response (and behaves fearfully).

Trigger-Treat Techniques: Another application of this same concept (classical conditioning) is used when we attempt to change an unpleasant association (fear, anxiety) to one that is neutral or even, if possible, pleasurable. For example, redirection techniques that rely upon building a "trigger-treat" association are frequently used with dog-reactive dogs to change what was an unpleasant association (sight of unfamiliar dog predicts fear/anxiety) to an association that is either neutral/relaxed or in the best of all worlds (though admittedly, not easy to achieve), is actually pleasurable. An example of this is a dog who has learned to react with excessive barking and aggression towards unfamiliar dogs who approach while he is out walking on lead with his owner. A "trigger-treat" protocol to attempt to change this behavior involves careful exposure to other dogs who approach outside of the dog's trigger distance. When the dog first notices the other dog (the trigger), the owner quickly redirects with a very high value treat. This sequence (trigger-treat), over time, links the sight of another dog with a pleasurable (eating) response, with the intent of reducing or eliminating the dog's prior response of anxiety or fear.

Considering Dogs' Emotional States: So, how do research studies about contrived emotional states relate to touch-then-treat and trigger-then-treat training techniques? Well, consider that trainers and behaviorists pay very close attention to the timing that we use with these techniques. Traditionally, most ascribe to the premise that the sequence that each stimulus occurs is essential for effective learning to take place. For example, in the "touch-then-treat" method for teaching dogs to accept handling, the treat should immediately follow the touch so that handling reliably predicts presentation of the treat. This approach results in the neutral stimulus (touch) ultimately taking on the same emotional attributes as the unconditioned stimulus (treat). Because dogs who are eating treats are usually happy dogs and because dogs (like humans) learn associations very quickly and efficiently, this conditioning leads to dogs who tolerate and often enjoy all types of handling. Similarly (though admittedly more challenging), in trigger-then-treat, the treat should come immediately after the dog becomes aware of, but has not yet reacted to, the unfamiliar dog (the aversive stimulus). This timing can be pretty darn difficult for many owners (and even for trainers) as we may treat too late or not at all (or are forced to back out of the situation altogether to avoid an unpleasant response in the dog). Treating too late when trying to counter-condition a reactive dog is especially ineffective and problematic.

Okay but what about treating *too early*? If we are to believe the research that we just reviewed, it may actually be helpful to treat *before* the touch or the trigger, as this could be used to induce a relaxed and happy emotional state in our dogs. Think about how your dog behaves when you share a treat with him for no reason, or when you give her a biscuit after she comes in from an outing. Most people would agree that dogs enjoy treats and that giving them a highly valued biscuit or dog treat naturally induces happiness and pleasure. So, dogs who are being given a yummy treat are happy dogs. Agreed?

Happy State of Mind = Favorable Perceptions: The research suggests that inducing a positive emotional state, even arbitrarily (smiling or waving a thumb's up gesture) puts a person in a state of mind that influences their perceptions of subsequent events in a favorable way. Applying this to dog training; if we purposefully induce a pleasurable emotional state *before* our dogs need to make a decision about another stimulus (i.e. being handled or reacting to an unfamiliar dog), might we also improve their overall perceptions of (i.e. reaction to) that stimulus? This is essentially the doggy version of "*George is a good guy; he was forced to behave badly by a difficult situation*". Practically speaking, perhaps we could enhance the effectiveness of the touch-then-treat and trigger-then-treat techniques by adding some "pre-stimulus conditioning"; a change that would also allow us to relax a bit regarding the timing used with these techniques.

The Hypothesis: Dogs who are induced to experience a pleasurable emotional state (i.e. calm, happy, relaxed) are expected to respond more rapidly and successfully to classical conditioning techniques (touch-then-treat and/or trigger-then-treat), that are dogs who are not so induced. The next step in the scientific method is to design a study to actually test this hypothesis with a group of dogs.

3
Your Face is Gonna Freeze Like That...
(The Study)

What are study groups, why do we need controls, and by the way, who is Steve?

The mental manipulations that we described earlier are actually a type of *psychological priming*. Priming occurs when the way in which a person responds to an event (technically called a stimulus) is influenced by previous events. Perhaps most intriguing is the fact that much of this influence takes place outside of our brain's conscious awareness. So, when applied to dog training, a working hypothesis is that priming may work with dogs; specifically priming dogs to feel happy and relaxed will enhance learning during touch-then-treat.

Can a Dog's Emotional Responses and Behaviors be Primed?
Like most people who live with and love dogs, my intuitive response is "*Of course they can*"! But, intuitions aside, if we are being good canine scientists, how might we collect actual data that either supports or refutes this hypothesis? Let's start with my friend Terry and her dog Steve.

The Steve Study: Terry sets up a study protocol of daily training sessions with Steve. In each session, Steve is primed using a favorite food treat. Terry decides to use 10 repetitions of reinforcing friendly eye contact, something Steve readily and regularly offers, as her priming stimulus. Each time that Steve offers eye contact, she gives him a high value food treat. Terry follows the priming portion of the session with a series of touch-then-treat exercises in which Steve's front paws, mouth, and ears are handled gently using the touch-then-treat training method. Terry repeats the entire routine once per day for a period of three weeks.

Data Collected: For each training session, Terry rates Steve's response to the three types of handling (ears, paws, mouth) using a five-point rating scale that ranges from "does not accept at all" (score of 1) to "accepts completely" (score of 5). This type of scale, called a "Likert scale" is commonly used in studies that rate subjective experiences. (For example, think of the rating scales that you may have used when completing surveys or exams). Terry scores Steve's responses before the experiment begins (pre-test) and daily (after each session; the post-test) until the end of the study. Here are Steve's mean (average) weekly scores, before (pre-) and after (post-) testing, for each handling exercise:

Steve's Mean (Average) Handling Scores over the 3-Week Test Period

HANDLING	PRE-TEST	WEEK 1	WEEK 2	WEEK 3
EARS	4.1	4.8	4.8	5.0
PAWS	1.4	3.5	4.2	5.0
MOUTH	2.1	3.2	4.4	4.4

Results and Conclusions: Steve's scores show that he was quite tolerant of having his ears handled at the start of the study. He had a high mean score of 4.1 out of 5.0. In contrast, Steve did *not* tolerate handling of his paws (mean score 1.4) or of his mouth (mean score 2.1) at the start of Terry's study. All three areas of handling showed improvement over the 3-week training period. By the end of Terry's study, Steve completely accepted Terry's handling of his ears and paws and showed a great deal of improvement in allowing Terry to work with his mouth. Terry concluded that *"priming is an effective training tool that leads to improvement in a dog's acceptance of handling exercises"*

Is Terry justified in this conclusion? Does Steve's response tell you if priming enhanced classical conditioning (touch-then-treat training) in dogs? In a word, **NOPE**.

There are several problems with using a **Steve Study** (or a Muffin study, or a Rover study or a Cooper study). Some of these may be immediately obvious to you; others perhaps less so. Here are four reasons that Steve's response (though very nice for Steve and Terry) should not be used to make conclusions about our hypothesis:

1. **Confounding factors:** Several other factors may have influenced Steve's behavior. The passage of time alone (especially in an adolescent dog) may have caused Steve to more readily accept handling. Steve may also have started to tolerate handling regardless of any type of training intervention, simply in response to the daily scheduled interactions with Terry. Finally, his response may have been due to touch-then-treat alone, regardless of priming. These multiple uncontrolled factors are expressly why all studies need to include one or more control groups.

2. **Experimenter bias:** Terry was not blinded to the treatment and had expectations that it would be effective. This leads to a common cognitive error called **confirmation bias**). In this case, Terry's bias is also caused by a placebo effect and would lead her to err on the side of seeing improvement where it may not have actually existed.

3. **Steve ain't stable**: No, this is not a derogatory statement about Steve. What I mean is that Steve, like all biological creatures, varies in his day-to-day behaviors. That variation, which occurs both within an animal and between animals,

must be accounted for when trying to determine if an animal is actually responding to a treatment or if the results that we are seeing are purely by chance and are caused by normal day-to-day fluctuations. In this case, the fluctuations are in behavior or learning, but this applies to all biological processes.

4. **One Steve = Anecdote (not a study)**: Last but not least, the fact that Steve varies day-to-day in his behavior is further complicated by the fact that ALL dogs vary from one another (we all know this, of course). In this particular case, we would expect that dogs vary in the degree to which they respond to priming (if priming does indeed work). The trick with research is....here is the punch line......separating the normal variation that occurs within and among dogs from the variation that may be caused by our treatment (in this case, priming). This need to partition variation into its various sources explains both why we need to study **groups** of dogs and why we always need one or more of those groups to be a **control group**. This is also the reason that we need statistics - to keep us from making incorrect conclusions that occur because Steve just happens to be an unusually smart dog (which of course, he is), because of normal differences among dogs, or because Steve just happens to be having a good month.

Instead of testing our hypothesis on just a single Steve, we actually need to test it on a sample of the entire population (i.e. multiple Steves). So, should we go out and find a group of 26 young, male, Border Collies? Probably not (unless we intend to make conclusions about priming that apply only to young, male BCs). What we need is a sample of dogs that is representative of all dogs in the population. To make certain that the results we see reflect a true treatment effect (or the absence of an effect) we need to test our hypothesis on a study group that is a sample of dogs that is **representative** of the population of dogs that we would like to make conclusions about. So, if we intend to make

26

conclusions about young adult dogs living in homes, we must select a group of dogs that are one year of age or older, are of various breeds (and mixes) and that include males and females.

We advertise our study through local veterinary clinics and after several weeks, have identified a group of 75 dogs and owners who would like to participate in our study. We now have our study group. The next study design question to ask is: What are the treatment and control groups that are needed for our study? To thoroughly control this study, we need three groups:

1. **Treatment (Experimental) Group**: Also called the "test group", this is the group of dogs that will receive the experimental treatment; in this case this is a series of Priming + Touch-then-Treat training over a period of three weeks (25 dogs or n = 25).

2. **Positive Control**: Positive control groups are used when we need a control that is expected to have a positive result, allowing the researcher to show that the protocol was capable of producing results above and beyond what was expected in the absence of the treatment. In our study, this would be a group of dogs who are not primed, but are still trained to accept handling using *Touch-then-Treat only*. (n = 25)

3. **Negative Control**: Negative control groups are used to make sure that no confounding variables affect results and to factor in any likely sources of bias. A negative control can also be a way of setting a baseline. In our study, the negative control will be dogs who received no training at all. *No training*. (n = 25)

Study Protocol: Dogs are randomly assigned to one of these three groups. (We might also "block" dogs across treatments, a technique that matches dogs by sex, age, breed or other sources of variance that we wish to control). We use the same daily training procedures and schedule that Terry used in her study, with one exception. The person who will score each dog after their daily training (or no training session) with Terry, is **not Terry.** Rather, we will use a scorer who is "blinded" to the study treatments and is present only to score each dog's response to handling, with no knowledge of the treatment group that the dog is in.

In the final part of the *"Face is gonna freeze"* series, we will look at a set of fictional data that were collected from the study along with some of the conclusions we might make from our hypothetical study. For now though, you may be asking......Why is this approach important? Well, let me tell you.......first gotta climb.....

Up on my Soapbox

Testing new ideas using the scientific method protects us from making Steve Study mistakes. Sure, you may see improvements in your dog's coat, vitality, agility performance, or health when you switch him from a cooked to a raw diet, when you decide to go grain-free, when you train him to balance his front feet on a ball, or when you use the ointment for his ear infection that Joe next door (who happens to know a lot about dogs) concocted for you.

However, without adequate study that includes groups of subjects, control groups, blinded (i.e. unbiased) observers and statistical analysis, you cannot know if something that has not yet been studied is actually doing what you think (or hope.....remember the dangers of confirmation bias) that it is doing. While not infallible, the scientific method is constructed to prevent or minimize bias, to test sample groups that represent a population, and to prevent us from coming to conclusions based only upon our desires, beliefs or intuitions, or according to our dear beloved, and yes, very smart dog, Steve.

4
Your Face is Gonna Freeze like that.......
(Why We Need Multiple Steves)

Chihuahuas to Great Danes; The importance of sampling and recognizing normal variation among dogs

---

Our hypothetical "Steves" study consists of three groups of dogs; the treatment group, the positive control group, and the negative control group. Each group consists of 25 young adult dogs, representing a range of breeds and breed-types. This collection of dogs is considered a *sample* of the population that we are testing. For this study, we define the population as all young adult dogs living in homes.

It's All about Variance: Let's start by all agreeing that dogs vary. They come in different sizes, breeds, personalities, with diverse past experiences and of course with a wide range of home lives and owners. Individuals also vary in their rate of learning, interest in different games and tricks, and motivation and talent for dog sports. It is exactly these differences that require the use of both a representative sample of dogs (rather than a single Steve) and the use of statistics to analyze study data to produce results.

Let's Illustrate this Concept with....Dogs, of Course: For any given measure (for example, height at the withers, coat length, degree of territorial behavior, or as in our current example, tolerance of handling) the ways that individual dogs vary is measured with a statistic aptly called *variance.* Variance is then used to calculate a numerical measure called a *standard deviation.* Standard deviations (SD) and their close cousin, *standard errors,* provide an estimate of how much variability there is within and between groups of dogs around the mean (average) of a given measurement. The SD is affected by a number of things, one of which is the type of sample that we choose to use in an experiment. Let's say we chose two sets of samples for our study. The first set comes from ALL dog breeds (and mixes); let's call this the Chihuahuas to Great Danes Sample. The second group comes only from dogs who are members of the herding or sporting groups and who range in size from an average Border Collie to an average Golden Retriever. Below are the two different bell-shaped curves that represent the expected variance among individual dogs within each of the samples.

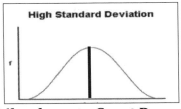

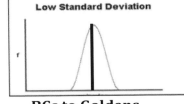

Chihuahuas to Great Danes   **BCs to Goldens**

Chihuahuas to Great Danes: When we study a sample of dogs that is representative of the entire dog population, the sample is expected to have relatively high variance (lots of spread around the mean, the vertical center line), which represents all of the naturally occurring differences among dogs of that population. In our example, the study of priming, this sample of dogs is expected to vary widely in terms of how well or poorly they accept having their feet, ears and mouths handled because it includes dogs with a wide range of temperaments, learning ability, and innate handling tolerances. The plus side of this type of sample is that we can make conclusions from it that applies to all dogs (not just the Steves of the world)! So, is there a down side? Well, unfortunately, yes. The greater the variance (spread around the mean), the more difficult it is to detect true differences that are caused by our treatment (in this case, priming) when they exist. Think of it as having a bunch of noise in the background that interferes with our ability to "hear" (measure) the effects of a particular treatment or intervention. This variability, while ac-

31

counted for using statistics, can make it relatively difficult to detect a treatment effect.

BCs to Goldens: We could of course select a less "noisy" sample (i.e. less spread around the mean). If our sample was restricted to include just herding and sporting breeds, the variability in responses would be smaller as there are fewer naturally occurring differences among individuals in this group. We would have an easier time detecting (statistically speaking) an effect of priming because the "noise level" of naturally occurring variance would be expected to be lower. The downside here - I am sure you are ahead of me on this one – herding and sporting breeds, beloved though they may be, are *not* representative of all dogs. We would be limited in the conclusions that we could (should) make from a study that used this sample.

Unfortunately, because this is real life, we do see studies in which samples are unrepresentative of the population that they are intending to study. Although the results of such studies can be helpful and can "push the peanut" of knowledge forward a bit, one must always be aware that the conclusions that can be made from a study's results must be within the parameters of the type of sample that was used in the study. (More about this later, in Essay 6 *"Thyroid on Trial"*).

For now, let's get back to our hypothetical study. What might we learn about the effects of priming from our *Study of Multiple Steves?* Following is a table showing the mean weekly scores for the two control groups and the treatment group for just the touching feet portion of the experiment. The ± after each mean is the standard deviation and as you now understand, this represents the "spread" of individual dogs' scores around the mean (average value) within each group. Below the table is a line chart showing the average change in "foot handling scores" for the three groups during the study period.

Group Mean (Average) Handling Scores over a 3-Week Test Period

GROUP	MEAN SCORES (WEEKLY) ± S.D.			
	PRE-TEST	WEEK 1	WEEK 2	WEEK 3
Negative Control (No training)	1.8 ± 0.34	1.7 ± 0.34	2.0 ± 0.34	2.2 ± 0.34
Positive Control (touch-treat only)	1.6 ± 0.31	3.0 ± 0.31	3.6 ± 0.31	4.0 ± 0.31
Test Group (Priming and touch-treat)	1.2 ± 0.36	3.4 ± 0.36	4.9 ± 0.36	4.9 ± 0.36

Line Graph of Group Handling Scores over a 3-Week Test Period

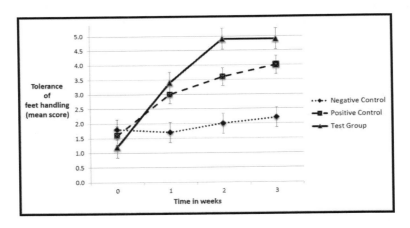

Results: What do the numbers in the table (mean values ± SD) and the line chart tell us? Well nothing (yet) without doing a further statistical test. We can use a statistics procedure called *repeated measures ANOVA* with this type of study design; a test that allows us to account for measuring "feet touch tolerance" in the same dogs on multiple occasions AND also compares the three groups to each other (pretty cool!).

The results of this statistical test tell us that:

1. Dogs with no training (negative control group; dotted line) did not show significant improvement in feet handling scores over the study period. Notice the relatively flat line going from the pre-test at week 0 to three weeks.

2. Dogs trained with either touch-treat alone (positive control; dashed line) and those trained with priming and touch-treat (test group; solid line) showed significant improvements in their feet handling tolerance over the three-week study period.

3. Dogs trained with priming plus touch-treat (solid line) had significantly higher (better) feet handling scores than dogs who had no training (dotted line) and compared to dogs trained with touch-treat training alone (dashed line). Notice the gaps between the lines and the steepest slope (incline) of the solid line.

What can We Conclude? We conclude that this study found that including priming prior to touch-treat training when teaching feet handling tolerance to young adult dogs significantly improved the success of the training procedure. And if our scores were similar for ears and mouths, we could include that priming is effective in those handling exercises as well. (NOTE: Remember that this study was hypothetical and has not actually been conducted....yet....this might be a nice project for a graduate student of animal behavior!)

And that, in a nutshell, is why we need Multiple Steves! Let's now take a more detailed look at control groups, most specifically the placebo group. Consideration of a placebo effect is especially important when we are evaluating a new approach to training our dogs, a new nutritional supplement or medication, or even something as simple as changing the food that we feed.

5
Consider the Placebo

A special type of placebo effect can influence an owner's interpretation of how well a particular diet, medication, or training procedure is affecting their dog.

Most people are familiar with the concept of a "placebo effect", the perception of improved health while unknowingly receiving a sham (placebo) treatment that in reality should have no benefit at all. Growing up, my mother referred to this as "giving someone a sugar pill". The assumption is that because we believe that we are receiving an actual treatment, our mind tells us that we should feel a bit better. Then amazingly, we do feel better. We notice a reduction in symptoms and ultimately conclude that the "medicine" must be working. The irony is that placebos actually can be powerful medicine (or something), at least for some people, for some diseases, some of the time.

Placebos and Us: The effects of placebos in human medicine are well-documented and are described with human diseases of almost every type. The highest level of placebo effect is seen with diseases that have subjective symptoms that are patient-reported and difficult to measure directly, that tend to fluctuate in severity, and that occur over long periods of time (i.e. are chronic). Examples of these are depression, anxiety-related disorders, gastric ulcer, asthma, and chronic pain. In medical research, an average placebo response rate of 35 percent is reported, with rates as high as 90 percent for some health conditions. By any standard, that is a whole lot of sugar pill response.

Although the reasons that we respond to placebos are not completely understood, medical researchers universally accept the importance of considering them when studying new treatments. Studies of new drugs or medical interventions include placebos

36

as control groups to allow unbiased comparisons with the treatment or intervention that is being evaluated. Any effect that the placebo group shows is subtracted from the effect measured in subjects who are receiving the actual medication. The difference between the two is considered to be the degree of response attributable to the treatment. If a placebo control group was not included, it would be impossible to differentiate between a perceived response (placebo) and a real response to the treatment. Today, double-blind, placebo-controlled clinical trials are considered to be the "Gold Standard" of study designs by medical researchers. The "double-blind" part refers to the fact that in addition to having both a placebo group and a treatment group, neither the researchers nor the subjects know which subjects are getting the treatment and which are getting the placebo.

What about Dogs? Can a placebo effect occur with dogs? Possibly, but things work a bit differently where our dogs are concerned. Most obviously, while highly communicative in many ways, dogs cannot specifically tell us what part of their body is in pain, how intense that pain is, if it is abating, or by how much. Rather, we use our knowledge of a dog's behavior and body language to determine how he is feeling. As their caregivers, we are the recorders and the *reporters* of our dogs' health, symptoms, and response to treatments. Similar to human studies, this is most relevant when the symptoms are things that are not easily measured using medical tests and that are more subjective in nature.

A second important difference is that dogs are basically always blinded to treatments. Although they may understand that something different is being done to them (or that there is a strange pill buried in that piece of cheese), most people will agree that dogs do not have an understanding that they are being medicated for a particular health problem or are on the receiving end of a new behavior modification approach. As a result, unlike human patients, dogs lack the specific expectations and beliefs about health interventions that may be necessary for a placebo effect to occur directly. However, because it is the *owner* who reports many symptoms and changes in health to their veterinarian and also who conveys subjective information regarding the dog's response to a given treatment, a different type of placebo effect may be in action with dogs. This is called a "caregiver placebo effect". As with human maladies, the conditions for which this type of placebo effect has been described in dogs are those that involve subjective measures of health (pain, activity level, appetite) and that have a tendency to fluctuate in severity. Let's look at two examples – the caregiver placebo effect in dogs with osteoarthritis and in dogs with epilepsy.

Does Your Dog Hurt Less? Osteoarthritis is a painful and progressive health problem that can seriously impact a dog's quality of life. A variety of medical and nutritional treatments are available today for afflicted dogs. These range from NSAIDS (ex. deracoxib, meloxicam), nutrient supplements (ex. glucosamine, chondroitin sulfate) to alternative medicine approaches (acupuncture, cold laser therapy). Researchers who have studied these treatments use subjective measures of lameness in which dogs' owners and veterinarians numerically rate their dog's degree of pain, mobility, and interest in daily activities in response to treatment. Some, but not all, studies also include objective measurements of arthritis that quantify the amount of weight bearing in the affected legs and weight distribution in the body.

Arthritis Study: In virtually *all* placebo-controlled studies of this type, a substantial proportion of owners and veterinarians have reported improvement in the placebo-treated dogs. However, when measured using weight-bearing techniques, the dogs in that group showed no change in or a worsening of disease. Michael Conzemius and Richard Evans at the University of Minnesota's College of Veterinary Medicine decided to quantify the actual magnitude of the placebo effect in this type of experimental trial (1). They analyzed the data from 58 dogs who were in the placebo control group of a large clinical trial that was testing the effectiveness of a new NSAID. All of the enrolled dogs had been diagnosed with osteoarthritis and had clinical signs of pain and changes in gait and mobility. This was a multi-centered design, which means that each dog's own veterinarian conducted the bi-weekly evaluations of gait and lameness. Both owners and veterinarians completed questionnaires that measured whether the dog showed improvement, no change, or worsening of arthritis signs over a 6-week period. Neither the owners nor the veterinarians knew if their dog was receiving the placebo or the new drug.

Results: Half of the owners (50 %) stated that their dog's lameness decreased during the study, 40 percent reported no change, and 10 percent said that their dog's pain had worsened. When these reports were compared with actual change as measured by force platform gait analysis, the caregiver placebo effect, (i.e. thinking that improvement occurred when there was either no change or an actual worsening of signs), occurred in *40 percent of owners*. The veterinarians performed no better. A placebo effect occurred 40 to 45 percent of the time when veterinarians were evaluating dogs for changes in gait or pain. This means that not only were the owners strongly invested in seeing a positive outcome, so too were their veterinarians. This effect occurred despite the fact that all of the human participants were aware of the 50 percent chance that their dog was in the placebo group, not the drug group, and that there was no way to be certain which group their dog was in.

Seizure Study: This study used an approach called a "meta-analysis" which means that the researchers pooled and then reexamined data collected from several previous clinical trials (2). Veterinarians from North Carolina State University College of Veterinary Medicine and the University of Minnesota reviewed three placebo-controlled clinical trials that examined the use of novel, adjunct treatments for canine epilepsy. During the treatment period owners were asked to record all seizure activity, including the length of the seizure, its intensity, and the dog's behavior before and immediately following the seizure. The pooled results showed that the majority of owners of dogs in the placebo group (79 %) reported a reduction in seizure frequency in their dog over the 6-week study period. Almost a third of the owners (29 %) said that there was a decrease of more than 50 percent, the level that was classified in the study protocols as indicative of a positive response to treatment.

What's Going On? Well, several things, it appears. The most obvious explanation of the caregiver placebo effect in dogs is owner expectations of a positive response when they assume an actual treatment is being administered to the dog. Whenever we introduce a new medication or diet or training method and anticipate seeing an improvement in our dog's health, nutritional well-being or behavior, we naturally tilt toward seeing positive results and away from seeing no change (or worse – a negative effect). This is a form of *confirmation bias* – seeing what we expect to see and that confirms our preexisting beliefs. In fact, an early study of the caregiver placebo effect in dogs found that when owners were asked to guess which group their dog was in, the owners who said that they were certain that their dog was in the treatment group (but was actually in the placebo group) demonstrated the strongest placebo effect (3).

Such expectations may be an especially strong motivator when we are dealing with maladies that have affected our dog for a long time, infringes upon the dog's ability to enjoy life, and for which we feel that we are running out of options. Osteoarthritis and seizure disorders were the health conditions studied in these papers, but I can think of several other problems with our dogs for which we may easily succumb to the power of the placebo effect. These include chronic allergies, adverse reactions to food ingredients, anxiety-related behavior problems and even cancer.

Cognitive Dissonance: Another factor that may contribute to the caregiver placebo effect is finding oneself in a state of contradiction. When we invest time and money (and hope) into a new treatment for our dogs, it follows that we will naturally have high expectations that the treatment will work. Indeed if it does not, we may experience cognitive dissonance, the uncomfortable feeling caused by holding two contradicting beliefs in one's mind at the same time. For example, *"I was told that giving my dog dehydrated gooseberry rinds would cure his chronic itching; these rinds are expensive and hard to find. He does not seem any better...... This is not a good feeling...."* Psychologists tell us that our brain reduces this discomfort for us (without our conscious awareness, by the way) by simply changing our perceptions. In this case, convincing oneself that the dog does seem a bit less itchy, her coat is a bit healthier and overall, she does really seem to be feeling better, immediately solves this problem for the brain and for our comfort level.

The Hawthorne Effect: Finally, a related phenomenon that is common enough to have earned its own name is the Hawthorne Effect, also called observation bias. This is the tendency to change one's behavior (or in our case how one reports their dog's behavior) simply as a result of being observed. The Hawthorne Effect suggests that people whose dogs are enrolled in an experimental trial may behave differently with the dog because they know they are enrolled in a trial that is measuring many aspects of the dog's life. In the case of the arthritis studies, owners may have altered how regularly they exercised their dogs, avoided behaviors that worsened the dog's arthritic pain, or began to pay more attention to the dog's diet and weight. The point is that when people are enrolled in a research trial or are starting a new medical treatment, diet, or training program and are being monitored, they will be inclined to change other aspects of how they live with and care for the dog as well. These changes could be as important (or more important) than the actual treatment (or placebo). This is not necessarily a bad thing, mind you, and is another reason why we always need control groups, but the occurrence of the Hawthorne Effect emphasizes the importance of recognizing that the thing that we think is working for our dog may not actually be the thing that is doing the trick.

Take Away for Dog Folks: When trying something new with our dogs, might we, at least some of the time, in some situations, be inclined to see improvement when it does not truly exist? When interpreting our dog's response to a novel therapy or supplement or training technique are we susceptible to falling for the sugar pill? It seems probable, given the science. It is reasonable to at least consider the possibility that a placebo effect may be influencing our perceptions of our dog's response to a new food, a new supplement, a new training technique or a novel treatment. This is especially true if the approach that we are trying has not been thoroughly vetted by research through double-blind, placebo-controlled trials. While the development of new medications and foods and training methods is exciting and important, we must avoid the tendency to see improvement from something that is novel simply because we expect and desire it to be so.

CITED STUDIES:

1. Conzemium MG, Evans RB. Caregiver placebo effect of dogs with lameness from osteoarthritis. *Journal of the American Veterinary Medical Association* 2012; 241:1314-1319.

2. Munana KR, Zhang D, Patterson EE. Placebo effect in canine epilepsy trials. *Journal of Veterinary Internal Medicine* 2010; 24:166-170.

3. Jaeger GT, Larsen S, Moe L. Stratification, blinding and placebo effect in a randomized, double blind placebo-controlled clinical trial of gold bead implantation in dogs with hip dysplasia. *Acta Veterinaria Scandinavica* 2005; 46:57-68.

6
Thyroid on Trial
(Understanding the Evidence Pyramid)

Even in science, all evidence is not created equal.

Every day, we are bombarded with new information about dogs that arises from a variety of sources - via the internet, through our smart (or not so smart) phones, from our colleagues, friends and family, and of course from our neighbor Joe next door (who happens to know a lot about dogs). In this day and age of information overload, it should come as no surprise that deciding which information is trustworthy and which to view with a healthy dose of skepticism is increasingly difficult. Even in science, all evidence is not created equal. Luckily, we have a handy "evidence pyramid" to help us to sort the various categories of scientific study and to rate the types of information that they provide.

Interpreting the Pyramid: First, keep in mind that this pyramid graphic presents only *scientific evidence* and does not include the host of other types of information that we come across each day, such as anecdotes, testimonials, stories/experiences, and (non-expert) opinion. Second, as you move from the bottom to the top of the pyramid, the *amount* of information (published literature) decreases, but its relevance and reliability generally increases. Starting at the bottom:

- **Editorial and expert opinions**: Experts in a field will often produce textbooks and review papers that can provide a good foundation about the chosen topic. This information presents a helpful summary, but because it is not reporting results of a scientific study, cannot provide evidence that supports or refutes a new scientific hypothesis.

- **Case reports:** These are individual reports that are usually published by a practicing veterinarian. The "case" refers to one or more dogs with a condition who were found to respond to a particular treatment. People are often surprised that case reports are not regarded as strong scientific evidence. However, while case reports may generate new hypotheses, they cannot be used as strong support for an existing hypothesis because of their anecdotal nature and the lack of control groups (remember the Steve Series and the importance of considering the placebo effect).

- **Case-controlled and cohort studies:** Case-controlled studies occur when the researcher finds cases (dogs, in our example) that have the condition under question and then matches and compares those cases with other dogs who are similar, but lack the condition. Similarly, cohort studies compare large groups of dogs with or without a condition, over time. While providing a type of control, results of these studies are limited because showing a statistical relationship (usually correlation) between two groups does not mean than one factor necessarily caused the other.

- **Randomized controlled trials (RCTs):** This type of study is the most important and reliable source of scientific evidence.

It includes methodologies that use the scientific method, reduce the potential for bias (via randomization, blinding, and the use of placebos) and allows for comparison between intervention groups and carefully selected control groups.

- **Systematic reviews:** At the pinnacle of scientific evidence, this is a specific type of review in which experts in a field assess all of the relevant studies and the data (called a meta-analysis) that address a particular topic. Systematic reviews require enormous commitments of effort, time, and money and are only possible once a hypothesis has been studied in depth. Therefore, these studies are few in number, especially for many topics that are important to dogs.

Example - Thyroid on Trial: I recently came across a great example in the dog science literature of a hypothesis about canine health and behavior that progressed from a few initial case reports, through case-controlled studies and culminated with the gold standard - the completion of a randomized, controlled trial. The issue had to do with a common endocrine disorder in dogs, hypothyroidism, and its potential relationship with aggressive behavior.

Background Information: Thyroid hormone is produced by the thyroid gland. The active form of this hormone regulates cellular metabolism and so has effects in virtually all body systems. The condition of *hypothyroidism* refers to a reduction in thyroid hormone production and resulting clinical signs. Hypothyroidism generally develops in middle-aged or older dogs and certain breeds show a genetic predisposition. Documented clinical signs of hypothyroidism include lethargy, decreased interest in exercise, weight gain, changes to coat quality and hair loss, and skin problems such as seborrhea, hyperpigmentation and secondary bacterial infections.

Hypothesis: In recent years, it has been speculated that certain types of aggressive behaviors in dogs may be related to suboptimal or low thyroid hormone levels. Starting with case reports, this hypothesis has gradually worked its way up the evidence pyramid:

- **Case reports:** Two case reports were published in 2002 and 2003. Together, they involved a total of 5 dogs with owner-directed aggression, who were subsequently also diagnosed with hypothyroidism. The dogs responded to thyroid hormone replacement therapy with a reduction in aggressive episodes, leading to the hypothesis that *some cases of aggression in dogs may be associated with hypothyroidism* (1,2).

- **Case-controlled studies:** A case-controlled report was conducted a few years later (3). Records of over 1500 dogs were reviewed. Of these dogs, 61 percent were classified as either hypothyroid or with suboptimal thyroid function. A statistically significant correlation was found between thyroid dysfunction and dog-to-human aggression in this group of dogs ($p < 0.001$). However, two subsequent case-controlled studies failed to find a connection between thyroid hormone levels and behavior problems (3,4). *Conflicting results – jury still out.*

- **The Randomized Controlled Trial (RCT):** Most recently, in 2013, the connection between suboptimal thyroid hormone levels and aggression in dogs was examined using the Gold Standard of designs - a *double-blind, randomized, placebo-controlled study* (5). Dr. Nick Dodman and his colleagues at the Tufts Cummings School of Veterinary Medicine enrolled a group of 40 dogs, all of whom were exhibiting owner-directed aggression and were also diagnosed with suboptimal or low thyroid hormone levels. Following screening and a 2-week pre-treatment (baseline) period, the dogs were randomly assigned to either the treatment group (thyroxine replacement therapy) or to the control group (placebo). Neither the researchers nor the owners knew which group each dog was assigned to. Dogs were medicated twice daily for a period of 6 weeks. During both the baseline period and throughout the study period, owners recorded the number and type of aggressive episodes that their dog exhibited.

Results: The highly specific inclusion criteria for the dogs in this study (aggressive dogs that had borderline or low thyroid function) coupled with difficulties associated with working with dogs with aggression problems led to a relatively small initial sample size (n = 40). In addition, attrition was high, due to owner non-compliance or other problems. The researchers reported the following results:

- **Frequency of aggressive behavior within groups:** The frequency of aggressive episodes significantly decreased in *both* groups from baseline levels over the six-week experimental period. Here is that famous placebo effect that you now understand so well!

- **Treated group vs. placebo group:** Owner-measured aggression did not differ between the treated group and the placebo group during the first five weeks of the study period. During the final week of the study (week six), dogs who were treated with thyroxine and had normalized serum thyroxine levels showed slightly lower frequencies of aggression when compared with dogs who were receiving the placebo, but this difference was not statistically significant ($p = 0.08$).

RCT = Gold Standard: The Randomized Controlled Trial is truly the "gold standard" of experimental studies for several reasons:

- **Methodology:** An RCT design reduces bias and allows relevant comparisons because a matched control group is used, treatments are randomly assigned, and neither the experimenters nor the subjects (in this case the owners of the dogs) know which treatment each dog is receiving. In addition, the inclusion of a placebo treatment (as opposed to simply not treating the control group at all) allowed the researchers to measure and account for a placebo effect (which clearly was important in this study).

- **Clinical trials using dogs in homes:** This study was a clinical trial, meaning that it was conducted with owned dogs living at home with their owners. This differs from studies conducted with dogs living in kennels (typically at a university setting or at a pet food company's kennel). If you remember back to The Steve Series, a cornerstone of the scientific method is selecting a study sample that is *representative* of the population that you will make conclusions about. Therefore, while we can control many of the "variables of life" with kenneled dog studies (making those studies much easier to conduct and to detect differences), such a sample is by definition, *less* representative of the population of dogs than is a sample that includes dogs living at home.

Challenges: In-home clinical trials with dogs are wrought with enormous challenges, all of which make it difficult to demonstrate real effects when they exist and which can require larger sample sizes to detect any true differences. These include:

1. **Variations in daily life**: Every owner lives with his/her dog in ways that are idiosyncratic to that person's demographics, lifestyle, and values. These differences all impact an owner's perceptions of his dog's behavior (in this example, displays of aggression) as well as a tendency to show a placebo effect.

2. **Dog differences:** Generally speaking, the differences among pet dogs enrolled in a clinical trial are going to be greater (spread more widely around the mean) than those among a group of kenneled dogs. The most obvious difference is the variability in living situations and daily routines among households. These are not present when studying a group of dogs who are housed under the same conditions and who experience the same daily routines. For a researcher, this means that being able to identify a treatment effect (in this

case, a measurable reduction in aggressive episodes in dogs treated with thyroid hormone), is much more difficult when studying dogs in homes compared with studying dogs in kennels.

3. **Owner perceptions and compliance:** When the owner is the data collector, which is sometimes the only feasible approach with in-home studies, there will be error (variability) introduced by the different perceptions among owners as well as by varying levels of compliance. Extreme non-compliance usually leads to removal from the study, but this too is a problem since removing subjects from an already limited sample will further reduce the power of the experiment (i.e. the ability to detect a true difference when it exists).

4. **Placebo effects:** As we have seen, the placebo effect is a real outcome that must be accounted for in dog studies. When owners are aware that their dog is enrolled in an experimental trial, even though they are blinded to the treatment that their dog is receiving, the mere participation in the study can influence their perspective of their dog's behavior and their judgment of possible effects or side effects of the treatment (that their dog may or may not be receiving). Including a placebo control group in a study that includes subjective measures of behavior (such as measuring the number and intensity of an aggressive response) is even more important since subjective scales are generally less reliable than objective measures.

Take Away for Dog Folks: The RCT that examined the effects of thyroid hormone replacement therapy on borderline or frankly hypothyroid dogs with owner-directed aggression showed a slight numerical reduction in aggression that was not statistically significant. As a result, the researchers concluded that thyroid replacement therapy could not be wholeheartedly recommended as a treatment for aggression in hypothyroid dogs and that additional studies of this type may be helpful to further examine this potential connection.

Personally, I think that this is also an excellent example of the progression of science from a set of initial case reports, followed by case-controlled studies, culminating in a randomized, controlled, clinical trial. An examination of the final study illustrates the enormous commitment of labor, time, and money that is required when conducting clinical trials as well as the importance of including placebos and double-blinding in scientific studies. Kudos to the investigators - not only for conducting what was clearly a very challenging clinical trial, but also for reporting informative negative results in a peer-reviewed journal.

CITED STUDIES:

1. Fatjó J, Stub C, Manteca X. Four cases of aggression and hypothyroidism in dogs. *Veterinary Record* 2002; 151: 547-548.

2. Dodds WJ, Aronson LP. Behavioral Changes Associated with Thyroid Dysfunction in Dogs. *Proceedings 1999 American Holistic Veterinary Medical Association Annual Conference*, pp. 80-82.

3. Carter GC, Scott-Moncrieff JC, Luescher AU, Moore G. Serum total thyroxine and thyroid stimulating hormone concentrations in dogs with behavior problems. *Journal of Veterinary Behavior* 2009; 4:230-236.

4. Radosta LA, Shofer FS, Reisner IF. Comparison of thyroid analytes in dogs aggressive to familiar people and in non-aggressive dogs. *Veterinary Journal* 2011;192:472-475.

5. Dodman NH, Aronson L, Cottam N, Dodds JW. The effect of thyroid replacement in dogs with suboptimal thyroid function on owner-directed aggression: A randomized, double-blind, placebo-controlled clinical trial. *Journal of Veterinary Behavior* 2013; 8:225-230.

7
What the Nose Knows

The dog's scenting ability is put to the ultimate scientific test at the tip of the evidence pyramid –
The systematic review.

In *"Thyroid on Trial"* we used an evidence pyramid to explore the various types of scientific studies that have been used to examine the hypothesis that there is a connection between hypothyroidism and aggressive behavior in dogs. We followed this example up through most of the levels of the pyramid, finishing at the penultimate level, the randomized, controlled trial.

At the tippy top of the evidence pyramid is the systematic review. As I mentioned in that piece, systematic reviews are somewhat of a rarity in canine science because they entail an enormous amount of work and time and because such reviews are only possible once there is a robust body of published information about a topic. So, I was quite delighted to find a newly published systematic review of a topic that many dog folks have an interest in - *Canine scenting ability.*

What Does the Nose Know? It is generally accepted that dogs possess a phenomenal sense of smell. These talents are regularly demonstrated in the many ways that dogs work and play at various scenting tasks. Dogs are trained to find illicit drugs, explosives, and land mines for the police and military, to identify the presence of mold, insects and toxins in homes and public buildings, and in recent years, to diagnose the presence of cancerous tumors or changes in blood glucose levels in human patients (see Essay 32, *"The Sniff(th) Sense"* for more about dogs and cancer detection). On the recreation side of things, anyone who enjoys tracking or canine nose work with their dog knows that these canine sports are not only interesting and enjoyable for owners, but are great fun for the dogs as well.

Evidence in support of the dog's keen scenting ability comes from many sources, each of which is associated with varying degrees of reliability. Information ranges from anecdotes ("*Fluffy detected Aunt Marge's diabetes and saved her life!*"), to media reports of heroic finds and rescues, to controlled scientific studies. The diversity of the dog's olfactory talents is also expressed by the wide range of items that dogs can be trained to locate and identify.

The Systematic Review: Knowing this, a group of researchers at Freie University's College of Veterinary Medicine in Berlin, Germany conducted a systematic review of all of the published research regarding the domestic dog's ability to successfully detect selected odors. They published their results in the peer-reviewed journal, *Applied Animal Behaviour Science* in late 2013. Here is what they found:

- **Papers:** A group of 31 papers was initially identified. Of these, two were excluded for duplication and 15 were excluded because they did not meet the criteria for a systematic review (i.e. they did not include original research). This left 14 published studies for the review.

- **Odor substrates**: Biological substances were used in all of the studies. These included termites/ants (2), cancers (7), tree snakes (1), microbial growth (1), parasitic infection (1), bird/bat carcasses (1), and estrus in cows (1).

- **Training methods:** All of the studies used reward-based training methods. Five of the papers specifically mentioned that clicker training was used. One paper reported that using positive reinforcement to train dogs resulted in greater sensitivity to the test compound than that observed in an earlier study that had used aversive stimuli to train dogs to detect the same compound.

- **Duration of training:** Training period durations ranged from just a week to more than a year. While the authors assumed that more difficult tasks or training dogs with no previous training may have resulted in the more extended training periods, this was difficult to ascertain given the small number of studies and the limited information that was provided.

- **Trainer's experience/skills**: Most of the studies did not report the trainers' qualifications or experience, making it impossible to evaluate the impact of training skills upon success. Because a trainer's qualifications are expected to impact training duration and success, the authors note that this is an area in which additional study is needed.

Success Rates: Sensitivity and specificity were calculated in 6 of the 14 studies (see Essay 14 *"This Test You Keep Using"* for a detailed explanation of these two measures) and response rate (number of correct finds) was reported in 8 of the 14 studies:

- **Sensitivity:** Dogs' sensitivity (ability to correctly identify positive samples) ranged between 88 percent and 100 percent.

- **Specificity:** Dogs' specificity (ability to correctly identify negative samples) ranged between 91 percent and 99 percent.

- **Number of correct indications**: Dogs correctly found or indicated a positive sample 35 percent to 98 percent of the time.

- **Summary:** These results suggest that dogs are capable of successfully detecting and indicating a variety of biological substances, ranging from different forms of cancer, to insect or reptile infestations, to carcasses and biological states.

Study Limitations: All of the published studies had one or more limitations. While these do not invalidate the positive results, they do suggest the need for future research that is well controlled, blinded, and which includes multiple samples.

- **Blinding:** Only 6 of the 14 studies used methodologies that blinded handlers and researchers to sample type and position. Lack of blinding may cause handlers or researchers to inadvertently influence or interpret a dog's behavior.

- **Sample replicates:** Only three of the 14 studies reported using more than a single positive sample (i.e. replicate) during testing. A lack of replication prevents the measurement of sampling error, which is an important criterion when attempting to quantify successful odor detection. In addition, while 8 studies reported using different samples during training and testing, the remaining 6 did not include information about sample reuse so it is not known if different samples were used during training and testing in those studies.

- **Consistency:** Only four of the 14 studies met the most important evidence-based science criteria of being double-blinded, measuring test sensitivity and specificity, and using unique samples during testing. However, these four studies varied in methodologies, types of detection, and training durations of the dogs, making it difficult to compare results.

Take Away for Dog Folks: This systematic review shows that dogs can be successfully trained to detect a wide range of biological substances and that training methods that focus on positive reinforcement are the approach of choice for this type of training. In addition to providing a thorough review of a topic, systematic reviews also function to identify gaps in the research that may require additional study. In this case, further exploration of the specific methods and durations used to train scent detection work in dogs along with careful blinding to prevent handler signaling or sample contamination appear to be needed. Personally, I found it to be very exciting that 31 papers were found on the topic of scent detection work in dogs, 14 of which met all of the (rather strict) criteria for a veterinary medicine evidence-based review, and that of these 14, the majority reported successful or highly successful scenting responses in the dogs.

Now that you are a well-schooled citizen scientist, let's move on to the essence of *"Beware the Straw Man"*, taking a careful and scientifically critical look at many of our common beliefs about canine behavior, training, and the relationships that we have with the dogs that we love so much. We begin Part 2 of the book with a second look at our dog's sense of smell and what recent studies at a dog cognition laboratory in New York are teaching us.

CITED STUDY:

Johnen D, Heuwieser W, Fischer-Tenhagen C. Canine scent detection - Fact or fiction? *Applied Animal Behaviour Science* 2013; 148:201-208.

Part 2 - Behavior

8
Smell This!

New research examines how dogs use their noses when making decisions during their everyday lives.

Most dog folks would agree that the dog's nose is a pretty amazing sense organ. Indeed, we capitalize on the dogs' olfactory (smellin') acuity when we train them to select scent articles in Utility training, follow a missing person's trail, find contraband and other nasty stuff in public places, and even detect the presence of cancer in human patients. Research in recent years has shown us that the dog's impressive smelling abilities are due to a number of pretty cool physical adaptations:

Lots of Cells: Dogs have hundreds of millions of olfactory receptor cells lining the inside of their nose; many times more than the number found in the human nose. This difference contributes to their ability to detect almost impossibly minute concentrations of compounds. This large number of canine olfactory cells is enough to cause smell envy in any dull-nosed human.

Big Brain: Two parts of the dog's brain that interpret incoming information from the nose are the olfactory bulb and the olfactory cortex. Both of these areas are highly developed in dogs and are important for how dogs use the sensory information that the nose provides.

Sniff Sniff: Dogs sniff. We don't (at least not in the same way that they do). Canine sniffing involves a disruption of the dog's normal breathing pattern and functions to enhance a dog's ability to detect and differentiate smells. Here is what we currently understand about sniffing: First, as the dog inhales during a sniff, the air is diverted into several flow paths. This partitioning effectively increases the number of sensory cells within the nose that inhaled components are exposed to, increasing olfactory sensitivity. Then, during the exhale phase of the sniff, the air leaves via the dog's "side-nostrils", not out the front of the nose as it does with normal breathing. (So that's what those slits in the side of my dog's nose are for! Who knew?). Exhaling through the "side nose" is presumed to prevent the dog's sensory cells from being repeatedly exposed to the same compounds, thus slowing the process of scent habituation. (Consider how you no longer can smell "wet dog" after being around it for a while; that's scent habituation).

Choice by Smell: A group of researchers at Barnard College's Dog Cognition Laboratory, in New York City asked a broad question about the dog's olfactory ability: "*How do pet dogs use their nose to make decisions and choices in their everyday lives?*" Alexandra Horowitz, Julie Hecht and Alexandra Dedrick began the series of studies by first asking if dogs have the ability to discriminate between large and small concentrations of smells (1). This was of interest because previous work has shown that, similar to many primate species, dogs can visually discriminate between different quantities of food (2). It follows that, since the dog's nose is so spectacularly talented, that they would be at least equally capable of the same type of discrimination using their noses. Here is a summary of their clever research study:

Study Design: A group of 69 pet dogs (and their people) were recruited for the study. Following some initial pre-training to acclimate the dogs to the setting and test procedure, the dogs were presented with two covered plates, set equidistant apart. One plate held a single chunk of hotdog. The second, the mother lode plate, held five chunks of hotdog. In the first trial, dogs were given no guidance at all from their owner and were allowed to choose one of the two plates. (Because the plates were covered, the dogs were compelled to choose using only their sense of smell). In a second trial, designed to test for the effects of social cues, the owner demonstrated a clear preference for the plate holding the single piece of food before their dog was allowed to make his or her selection.

Results: There are actually a number of interesting findings (and additional questions) that came out of this paper. Two that seem to be especially relevant to dog folks are:

1. **Size did not matter**: The dogs in this study, pet dogs that had no previous training in any type of scent detection or scent following work, did not demonstrate an ability to discriminate a "small quantity" from a "large quantity" of food using only their sense of smell. This result is surprising, since dogs do seem to have this ability when tested using vision and considering what we know about dogs' highly developed olfactory acuity.

2. **Social cues did matter:** When owners demonstrated a clear preference for the plate that held the smaller quantity of food, the dogs did show a significant preference - for the plate with the smaller quantity! In other words, dogs were readily and easily influenced by the social cues provided by their owners regarding which plate to choose. This result was in agreement with earlier studies of visual preference - dogs of owners who pointed at a plate that clearly contained the smaller pile of food were more likely to choose that plate over the plate whose food runneth over!

Conclusions: The authors suggested that our dogs, living in a human-centered environment, may not always be using their noses to the extent of their actual ability. Perhaps when making decisions in everyday life dogs learn to depend too heavily upon social cues from their human companions, to the extent that they ignore information coming from their own senses.

Take Away for Dog Folks: The results from this study led me to think about how many of us live with our dogs and how we may unwittingly discourage them from using their noses on a daily basis. Perhaps by caring for our dogs so well, and making so many of their decisions for them (what to eat, when to eat, how much to eat, what plate to choose), we influence a bit too much and unintentionally inhibit one of their most amazing and enviable talents. For example, at my own training school we teach "*Leave it*", a command that can keep dogs safe when they decide to investigate something that may be dangerous to them. However, when we ask for this behavior, are we unintentionally inhibiting a dog's use of (and enjoyment of) his nose? Just a thought. Personally, I still will always teach this response to my dogs (and those of my students) because it is an invaluable behavior to train for its safety and control utility. However, reading this study has encouraged me to consider a bit more carefully each of the everyday circumstances in which I use it.

Consider also the currently popular K-9 Nose Work classes. Almost uniformly, reports about these scent work games are that dogs, (all dogs, regardless of their level of previous training, age, or athletic ability) love K-9 Nose Work and the success that they experience when encouraged to use their nose, search freely, and make independent decisions. Perhaps these classes are unleashing some of that latent "nose power" that all dogs have and that they may not always be encouraged to use when living in a typical anthropogenic (human-centered) world. So, Kudos to all of you who encourage your dogs to smell, sniff, find (safe) stuff, and who play nose games with your dogs, teach them to track, or simply regularly encourage them to "Smell This!"

CITED STUDIES:

1. Horowitz A, Hecht J, Dedrick A: Smelling more or less: Investigating the olfactory experience of the domestic dog, *Learning and Motivation* 2013; 44:201-217.

2. Prato-Previde E, Marshall-Pescini S, Valsecchi P: Is your choice my choice? The owner's effect on pet dogs' (*Canis lupus familiaris*) performance in a food choice task. *Animal Cognition* 2008; 11:167-174.

9
It's All Rock and Roll to Me

Does listening to music have a calming effect upon dogs?
If so, does the type of music that they listen to matter?

When training my dogs, I always have music playing. And, truth-be-told, my personal tastes gravitate neither to easy-listening nor to high-brow classical music. Rather, I am a rock n' roll gal, all the way home. On a given day, my dogs and I may be training agility to The Who, retrieving to Stevie Ray Vaughan, or practicing tricks to Ray Lamontagne. On days that my feminist freak flag is flying, Janis Joplin, Melissa Etheridge, and Alanis Morissette are on deck. My dogs of course are accustomed to this and (I hope) share my love of all that rocks. (Chippy, my Toller, seems to enjoy early Beatles).

So, considering my habit of training to music, I was interested to find a research study that examined the effects of music on dog behavior. In this case, rather than looking at dogs rocking out during agility training, the researchers were studying dogs housed in a kennel environment (1).

The Study: A kennel setting can be highly stressful for dogs, particularly those who are homeless and residing in a shelter. In attempts to improve their welfare, researchers have studied a variety of strategies for reducing kennel-induced anxiety. These include providing interactive toys, promoting social interactions with people, increasing opportunities for exercise and play, and adding various types of environmental enrichment. Sensory stimulation is a form of environmental enrichment that may use visual, olfactory, or auditory stimuli to induce a more calm and relaxed state. For example, there is ample evidence that listening to classical music has mood-enhancing effects in people and a small amount of evidence showing similar responses in dogs (2).

63

However, the effects of different genres of music have not been studied at all in dogs. For example, are they rockers like me or do they prefer muzak? Recently, a group of researchers at Colorado State University asked the questions: *"Can exposure to music during periods of kenneling reduce stress and anxiety in dogs?"* and *"Do dogs react differently to different types of music?"*

Dogs and Music Selections: Two groups of dogs were studied; adult Dachshund rescue dogs (n = 34) and owned dogs (multiple breeds), all housed in the same facility for short-term boarding (n = 83). The kennel was a traditional design consisting of a long row of indoor rectangular enclosures that faced each other on each side of a center concrete walkway. Dogs were housed either singularly or in pairs and were walked on-lead outdoors twice daily. Three types of music were tested: classical (4 selections), heavy metal (3 selections), and a commercial dog relaxation track (modified classical music). Music selections were played in a randomized sequence for 45-minute periods, with each period followed by 15 minutes of silence (no music). The control was a 45-minute period with no music. Dogs were observed by a single person (one of the scientists) for 5-minute periods throughout each music or control period. Recorded behaviors included the dogs' type of activity, time spent vocalizing, and the presence/absence of body shaking (an indication of fear or anxiety).

Results: Both the presence/absence of music and the *type* of music that was played influenced dogs' behavior and apparent stress levels and rescue dogs and boarding dogs responded similarly:

- **Activity:** Dogs spent significantly more time sleeping when listening to classical music than when they were listening to either heavy metal, the commercial relaxation music, or no music at all. Neither heavy metal nor the commercial relaxation track significantly affected sleep time or activity level. (Contrary to speculation, listening to heavy metal music did not induce hyperactivity; parents of teens, take note).

- **Vocalizations:** Both genre (music type) and song selection influenced vocalizations, although these effects were not dramatic. For example, dogs were silent for 95 percent of the time while listening to the classical selection, Moonlight Sonata. By comparison, they were silent just a bit less, 86 percent of the time, when no music was playing. In general, the kenneled dogs barked between 5 and 15 percent of the time and were *slightly* more inclined to bark when no music was playing.

- **Body shaking:** Dogs spent dramatically more time shaking when listening to heavy metal music (38 to 71 % of the time, depending on the selection) than when listening to classical music (0.5 to 2.8 % of the time), the commercial selection (0.5 %) or no music at all (1.2 %). One particular heavy metal song caused dogs to shake the most - a whopping 71 percent of the time. To put this in perspective, this means that, on average, dogs were showing nervous body shaking for 32 of the 45 minutes that they listened to this song.

Take Away for Dog Folks: Music appears to significantly influence the behavior of kenneled dogs, and this includes both rescue (homeless) dogs and dogs who are owned and are being temporarily boarded. This study provides some helpful information for trainers, owners, and shelter/rescue professionals alike:

- **Chill with Chopin**: Classical music apparently induces sleepiness in dogs (glad to learn that I am not alone in that respect). A response of increased relaxation/sleep is definitely a good thing for kenneled dogs, since anxious/stressed dogs are generally more active and spend less time relaxing than do non-stressed dogs.

- **Avoid the head bangers**: Heavy metal music is to be avoided with dogs as it appears to have induced stress, possibly severe stress, in kenneled dogs (again, good to learn, can't stand the stuff, myself).

- **Save your pennies:** The commercial selection that was tested in this study was marketed by the company selling it as being "psychoacoustically arranged" (whatever that means) to promote dog relaxation. However, this music had minimal effects on stress-related behavior in this study, performing less well than classical music that was not psycho-babble arranged. While the underlying cause for this difference was not clear, this result illustrates the risk of taking a bit of research (classical music is calming to humans) and applying it to dogs by marketing and selling a track of "relaxation music" without adequate supporting research.

The point should not be lost that the relaxation benefits of listening to classical music that are documented in humans (and now, documented also in dogs) may be of benefit to both shelter dogs and to the folks who care for them. So, even if you are an ol' time rock-n-roller, like me, consider at the very least, that classical music may be the way to go when you are working with group-housed dogs living in stressful environments.

CITED STUDIES:

1. Kogan LR, Schoenfeld-Tacher R, Simon AA. Behavioral effects of auditory stimulation on kenneled dogs. *Journal of Veterinary Behavior* 2012; 7:268-275.

2. Wells DL, Graham L, Hepper PG. The influence of auditory stimulation on the behavior of dogs housed in a rescue shelter. *Animal Welfare* 2002;11:385-393.

10
You Barkin' At Me?

Of the many ways in which dogs communicate with each other, how important is barking and what exactly are they saying to each other?

I have a ring tone on my mobile phone that I really like. It barks. Five barks (*bark-bark-bark-bark-bark*) for each ring. It is a real dog's voice, not a person fake-barking in that annoying way that certain people feel compelled to do when they see a dog. (Really, what is that about anyway?). Recently, my phone started barking while I was getting my hair cut. My hairdresser laughed and asked if any of my dogs react to the barking phone. I told him that no, they always ignore it, which is strange, since it is definitely the recording of a real dog bark. To which he replied *"Maybe the dog isn't saying anything"*.

Maybe. But recent research suggests that dogs do have something to say and that other dogs are often quite interested in hearing what that is.

A Bit of Background: The auditory (vocal) signals that animals make often have important communication functions and possess context-specific information. This means that a sound may be conveying information about several things at once. For example, an alarm call may vary in subtle but detectable ways depending on the location of the threat and how dangerous it is. Vocalizations may also be important signals that allow animals to recognize and identify other individuals. Indeed, this ability has been demonstrated in a wide range of species of birds, mammals, and even amphibians.

What about Dogs? Previous research has shown that like many other animals, the sounds that dogs make are varied and highly

67

context-specific and that humans, especially those who are experienced with dogs, are quite capable of distinguishing between different types of dog barks (1,2). However, while it is easy to test a human's response to dog barks (we can just ask them questions), it is more difficult to ask dogs what they are learning when they listen to the vocalizations of another dog. Difficult, but not impossible. A group of ethologists at the Eotvos Lorand University in Hungary designed two clever experiments in which they were able to ask dogs - *What are other dogs saying to you when they bark?*

Study Technique: The researchers used an approach called "habituation-dishabituation" to measure dogs' reactions to the recorded sounds of barking. The method works like this. The dogs were first allowed to habituate (i.e. become accustomed) to recordings of a particular dog who was barking in a particular situation. Habituation was measured by recording the number of seconds that the listening dog continued to show interest in a dog/situation combination over time. A decrease in attention was interpreted to indicate habituation. A dog would stop reacting to the sound as it lost significance much in the way we habituate to the sound of our air conditioner kicking on because it is heard repeatedly through the day.

Then (here is the clever part), the researchers changed either the identity of the dog who was barking or the context of the bark. The introduction of something that is new or unexpected should cause dishabituation, but only if the listener notices the change. (For example, if your air conditioner suddenly started making a rattling noise, you would dishabituate to it and take notice, right?). In this case, if the listening dog responded by suddenly increasing his/her attention to the recording, this means that the dog noticed the change and so was capable of distinguishing between different dogs and/or different causes of barking. If on the other hand, the change did not cause a change in the listening dog's behavior, such a result would indicate that the dog had habituated to the general sounds of a dog barking and was not gleaning any specific information from the recordings. The group of investigators published two studies with dogs using this technique.

Study 1: The researchers recorded the barks from five adult dogs in two different contexts; either in response to an unfamiliar person approaching a garden area or when left alone, tied to a tree in a park (3). They then brought 30 other dogs into the lab and played the recordings from a hidden recorder, first allowing habituation to a particular dog/situation and then, for the dishabituation test, changing either the dog who was barking or the cause of the barks.

Results: The subject dogs consistently showed an increase in interest to the recordings in response to both a change in identity of the dog who was barking and also in response to a change in the cause of barking. This suggests that dogs are capable of differentiating *who* is barking when they hear another dog and what the dog is barking about. What this study design could not provide however, is anything about the exact type of information (if any) that the dogs were gleaning from the recorded dogs or if they were capable of identifying a known individual by his or her bark.

Study 2: This time around, the researchers asked the question - *Do dogs recognize the barks of other dogs who they know and do they react to what their friends are barking about in a different way than how they react to a stranger's bark* (4)? A group of 16 dogs, all living in multiple-dog homes, were tested. The dogs were tested in their own homes (so had an attachment to the context) and they listened to a hidden recording of either an unfamiliar dog or of one of their housemate dogs (who was not present at the time, because that would just be weird). The two contexts for barking were the same - barking when left alone or barking at an unfamiliar person approaching the yard's fence. Each dog's reactions were videotaped to allow careful analysis of any changes in behavior while listening to the recordings.

Results: The dogs showed specific behaviors that depended upon who the barker was (friend or stranger) and upon what was causing the barking (isolation or territorial). Upon hearing a recording of their housemate, dogs would move toward the house where the dog was expected to be. Conversely, they moved toward the yard's gate when they heard the sound of an unfamiliar dog barking at a stranger. The listener dogs also barked most frequently in response to the "stranger coming" recordings, regardless of whether the bark came from their housemate or a stranger. The researchers concluded that dogs appeared to be able to identify other dogs "by bark" and that they also gained information about a bark's cause, simply by listening, in the absence of other cues such as the barking dog's body language or facial expressions.

Take Away for Dog Folks: The results of this study instruct us (once again) to take care with our assumptions when working with dogs. While it should be naturally obvious that dogs are proficient at recognizing and understanding one another via vocalizations and that a great deal of information is conveyed via barking (and I would bet a few of you were shaking your heads whilst reading and muttering, "well, no kiddin'"), we often do not *behave* as though we actually believe this to be true.

Here is what I mean. Dog owners, trainers and behaviorists frequently classify barking in dogs as a problem behavior. If we don't like it, if it annoys us, if we deem it excessive or an attention-seeking behavior, then it immediately gets dumped into the "behavior problem" bin. Well, granted, excessive barking can be annoying, can pose a community nuisance, and as a recurrent behavior may need some modifying. (Believe me, I understand vocal dogs - I live with a Toller). However, perhaps as humans we have become so intolerant of dogs barking that we may occasionally fail to see it for the important communication tool that it is in our efforts to stop it.

Up on my Soapbox

Up on the Ol' Box: Moreover, we may often get it wrong. Barking that is classified as problematic because it is thought to be "attention-seeking" could in actuality be a legitimate bid for affection from a chronically neglected dog. Or barks that an owner is instructed to ignore so as to "extinguish the behavior" may in fact be conveying true distress. (See Essay 23 "*Is it Time for the Extinction of Extinction?*" in Part 3 for more about this). Is it also not possible that a dog who shows alarm barking truly has something to be alarmed about? While I am not suggesting that we should allow all dogs, at all times, to bark to their little heart's delight (though, that is certainly what Chip my Toller is going for), I *am* advocating that just as we accept body postures, facial expressions, eye contact, elimination patterns, and touch (tactile signals) as important forms of communication in our dogs, so too we should accept (and decriminalize) barking.

As trainers and behaviorists, perhaps it is time to dial back the trend towards classifying any barking that an owner does not like as "attention seeking", "demand", or "nuisance" barking, and reclassify it as a normal communication pattern that warrants understanding of the cause and as needed, modification. As the very chatty species that we are, we should be sensitive to and wary of any training approach or behavior modification program whose goal is to produce a completely silent dog.

As for my barking phone, I will continue to enjoy it, even if the dog is speaking nonsense.

CITED STUDIES:

1. Pongracz P, Molna Cs, Miklosi A, Csanyi V. Human listeners are able to classify dog barks recorded in different situations. *Journal of Comparative Psychology* 2005; 119:228-240.

2. Pongracz P, Molna Cs, Miklosi A, Csanyi V. Acoustic parameters of dog barks carry emotional information for humans. *Applied Animal Behavior Science* 2006; 100:228-240.

3. Molnar C, Pongracz P, Farage T, Doka A, Miklosi A. Dogs discriminate between barks: The effect of context and identity of the caller. *Behavioural Processes* 2009; 82:198-201.

4. Pongracz P, Szabo E, Kis A, Peter A, Miklosi A. More than noise? Field investigations of intraspecific acoustic communication in dogs (*Canis familiaris*). *Applied Animal Behavioural Science* 2014; 159:62-68.

11
Mr. Licks-A-Lot

New information about the behavior of excessive licking and its possible connection to gastrointestinal problems

---

Do you live with a Mr. Licks-A-Lot? You know what I mean - a dog who, for reasons that he is not readily sharing, will suddenly and obsessively begin to lick the floor, the couch, the wall? Note that I am not referring to the dog who licks *you*, a behavior that usually communicates appeasement, affection, or in some cases, anxiety. Rather, the Mr. Licks-A-Lot that I am talking about is the dog who directs his obsessive licking primarily at inanimate objects.

Some dog folks, myself included, have associated a bout of this type of repetitious licking with stomach upset; and in the worst case scenario, as a reliable predictor of the impending vomit. An alternate explanation for excessive licking behavior in dogs is behavioral - specifically, that dogs who lick (a lot) may be experiencing anxiety, obsessive compulsive disorder, or age-related cognitive dysfunction. However, neither of these hypotheses had ever been studied scientifically. Until now.

The Study: A group of researchers at the University of Montreal Veterinary Teaching Hospital conducted a case-controlled study of dogs presenting to the hospital with excessive licking to surfaces (1). At the start of the study, owners completed a written history of the dog's behavior, which included the type of licking, its duration, frequency and intensity, and the occurrence of any signs of gastrointestinal (GI) disturbance. They also were required to videotape one or more licking episodes. Nineteen "licks-a-lot" dogs and 10 non-licking control dogs were enrolled in the study. All 29 dogs underwent complete gastrointestinal, behavioral and neurological diagnostic evaluations. When a gastrointestinal diagnosis was found, treatment that was specific to the disorder was initiated. When no diagnosis was found, a placebo treatment was used. All dogs were reexamined 30, 60 and 90 days later.

Results: Of the 19 dogs who presented with excessive licking, 10 of 19 dogs (53 %) exhibited clinical signs of GI disturbance, and 14 of 19 (74 %) were diagnosed with a GI disorder. Problems included several types of inflammatory disease, delayed gastric (stomach) emptying, chronic pancreatitis, gastric foreign body, and giardia infection. By comparison, only three dogs in the control group (30 %) were diagnosed with a GI problem. The difference in GI diagnosis frequency between the Mr. Licks-A-Lot group and the control group was statistically significant (74 % vs. 30 %, $p = 0.046$).

Following treatment, a reduction in both the frequency and the duration of licking behavior was reported in 59 percent of the affected dogs. Complete resolution of licking behavior was seen in 9 dogs (53 %). Note: The authors also reported that the study's internist saw clinical improvement in four additional dogs when evaluated at 120 to 180 days. Interestingly, anxiety was not related to excessive licking. Data collected through behavior profiles and video analysis found no differences in the degree of anxious behaviors shown by dogs in the licking group and dogs in the control group.

Take Away for Dog Folks: This study is the first to show that gastrointestinal disturbances may be the underlying cause of excessive licking of surfaces in dogs. Almost three-quarters of the dogs in this study were experiencing an undiagnosed GI disorder and more than half showed a complete cessation of licking behavior once the medical problem was resolved. The authors speculated that licking behavior may reflect feelings of nausea and/or abdominal discomfort in dogs. This new information does not eliminate the possibility that the underlying cause of excessive licking is behavioral in some cases. Rather, it suggests that the presence of an undiagnosed gastrointestinal disorder should be considered when a dog presents as a Mr. Licks-A-Lot and that we should avoid focusing on behavioral causes only when presented with this type of problem.

Addendum - Fly biting and Sandifer Syndrome: The same group of researchers published a case report that examined a possible connection between fly biting behavior in dogs and gastrointestinal disturbances (2). They studied 7 dogs who were presented for exhibiting snapping/jumping at imaginary flies using the protocol described above. All 7 dogs showed sudden head-raising and neck extension movements immediately prior to jaw snapping and the behavior was most pronounced or only occurred immediately after eating. Like excessive licking, fly snapping behavior in dogs is often classified as having a behavioral rather than a medical cause. Most commonly, it has been classified as a form of epilepsy (especially in Cavalier King Charles Spaniels) or as obsessive compulsive disorder. In this study, all seven dogs were diagnosed with a gastrointestinal problem and were subsequently treated. When reevaluated 30 days following the start of treatment, fly-biting had completely resolved in four dogs and had partially resolved in one dog.

Possible cause? The authors compare the behavior of these dogs with Sandifer Syndrome, a problem seen in human infants that is believed to be caused by gastroesophageal reflux or delayed gastric emptying. It was postulated that the characteristic movements of raising the head, extending the neck, and in dogs, snapping/gulping air serves to reduce esophageal or gastric discomfort. Although preliminary, this case report suggests that just as with excessive licking behaviors, gastrointestinal disease should be considered as a potential cause of imaginary fly biting behavior.

CITED STUDIES

1. Becuwe-Bonnet V, Belanger M-C, Frank D, Parent J, Helie P. Gastrointestinal disorders in dogs with excessive licking of surfaces. *Journal of Veterinary Behavior* 2012; 7:194-204.

2. Frank D, Belanger MC, Becuwe-Bonnet V, Parent J. Prospective medical evaluation of 7 dogs presented with fly biting. *Canadian Veterinary Journal* 2012; 53:1279-1284.

12
Fear Factor

Do fearful dogs experience greater risk of chronic health problems and a shortened life span?

Experiencing fear is not pleasant. Any human will tell you this. As one of our most basic emotions, fear functions as a rapid-fire means of communicating to our bodies "DANGER, DANGER - GET AWAY NOW!!" As a physiological state, fear is associated with a set of bodily changes that are decidedly uncomfortable. Respiration and pulse increase, we become hyper-vigilant of our surroundings, our hearts pound, and we may experience a strong inclination to flee.

Dogs who experience fear exhibit the same physiological signs as humans and most likely also suffer the same unpleasant emotional state. Common fears/anxieties in dogs include separation anxiety, fear of unfamiliar people or dogs, and sensitivity to thunder or loud noises. When these problems persist over long periods of time, they will definitely reduce a dog's quality of life and can negatively affect the relationship between the dog and his or her owner. In addition, long-term exposure to stress may affect dogs' physical health and longevity.

The Cost of Fear: There is evidence in humans and in laboratory species that experiencing prolonged periods of stress and anxiety increase an individual's susceptibility to disease and risk of premature death (1-3). A possible underlying cause for these unhealthy effects is thought to be chronic activation of the hypothalamic-pituitary-adrenal [HPA] axis, which is part of the body's natural defense against physical and psychological stressors. It is the HPA system that is responsible for elevated levels of cortisol, that well-known hormone that prepares one's body for flight or fight. Although cortisol is highly effective in the short-term, prolonged exposure to high circulating levels is associated with a number of chronic health problems, such as hypertension, insulin resistance, heart problems and immune disturbances. Increased oxidative stress also occurs during exposure to physical or emotional stressors, and is associated with an increased rate of cellular aging and death. Although the exact underlying mechanisms are not fully understood, it is well-established that living in fear is not good for us.

What about Dogs? Although the relationship between prolonged stress, health and lifespan is an active area of research in human subjects, until recently this association had not been studied in dogs.

The Study: Nancy Dreschel, a veterinarian at Pennsylvania State University, asked the question: "*Are dogs who are more anxious or fearful at increased risk for health problems and a shortened life span?*"(4). The study used a web-based questionnaire to collect information from people who owned a dog who had died within the previous five-year period. The survey included questions about the dog's demographics, social environment, behavior, training history, health, and daily interactions with the owner. A set of questions adapted from the validated C-BARQ program was used to collect detailed information about the presence or absence of fear-related and anxious behaviors. Each dog's age and cause of death were also recorded. The survey was available on-line for 7 months and resulted in 721 complete surveys that were used in the analysis.

Results: As one would expect, body size and weight were negatively correlated with lifespan. It is well-established that large/giant dogs have a shorter average life span than small and medium size dogs. In addition, neutered dogs had a longer lifespan than intact dogs and accidental deaths were associated with a younger age of death. When body size, neuter status, and accidental death were controlled for, several significant relationships were found between behavior and lifespan:

1. **Fear and lifespan:** A significant negative correlation was found between the fear of unfamiliar people and lifespan. This means that dogs who experienced a lifelong fear of strangers tended to die at a younger age than dogs who did not experience this type of fear. However, the earlier age of death in this subset of fearful dogs was not associated with any particular disease. (Because long-term activation of the HPA axis negatively affects the immune system, it was speculated that fearful dogs would be more susceptible to cancer, infections, or immune-mediated disorders. However, this relationship was not found in these data).

2. **Fear and skin health:** The presence of non-social fears (fear of new places or things) and separation anxiety were both positively associated with chronic skin problems. The underlying mechanism might be the effects of long-term stress on the immune system and skin health, a relationship that has been reported in human subjects. However, this study's design did not allow determination of causation, so conclusions regarding the underlying cause for this relationship could not be made.

3. **"Good" dogs and lifespan:** Lifespan was strongly and positively correlated with owner-reported "good" behavior. Dogs who were perceived as being well-behaved by their owner lived longer than those who were reported to be less well-behaved. Multiple factors may have been in play with this relationship. Because problem aggression was not specifically studied, euthanasia for aggression may have been a significant contributing factor. Less dramatically, owners who reported their dogs as less well-behaved may have been less bonded to the dog and more likely to euthanize at a younger age or to decline treatment for a serious illness. It is also possible that well-behaved dogs tend to live longer because they experience a less stressful and more harmonious home environment with their owner. Because none of these factors were studied separately, the exact cause or causes of this re-

lationship could not be teased out, but certainly warrants additional study.

Take Away for Dog Folks: Remember that survey studies provide information through the eyes of the owner and, in this case, the collected data were also retrospective (historical) in nature. These factors must always be considered when making conclusions about survey studies. In addition, the statistical tests used in this study tell us if two or more factors are related (i.e. correlated), but cannot provide information about the direction of that relationship or if there is another underlying cause that was not identified. Even considering these limitations, the results of this study suggest that prolonged fear and anxiety not only affect a dog's quality of life, but may also contribute to an early death and increased susceptibility to chronic health (skin) problems. Helping dogs to overcome fear is vital to improving their lives and our relationships with them. And, to those of you who are working with these dogs on a daily basis, thank you for all that you do.

CITED STUDIES:

1. Cavigelli SA, McClintock MK. Fear of novelty in infant rats predicts adult corticosteroid dynamics and an early death. *Proceedings of the National Academy of Science USA* 2003; 100:16131-16136.

2. McEwen BS. Stressed or stressed out? *Journal of Psychiatric Neuroscience* 2005; 30:315-318.

3. Schultz R, Beach SR. Caregiving as a risk factor for mortality. *Journal of the American Medical Association* 1999; 282:2215-2219.

4. Dreschel NA. The effects of fear and anxiety on health and lifespan in pet dogs. *Applied Animal Behaviour Science* 2010; 125:157-162.

13
Talking Turkey

Can supplementation with the amino acid tryptophan reduce problem aggression in dogs?

I grew up with a story-book grandmother. She was my mother's mom, "Nana" to my sister and me. As required of all perfect grandmothers, Nana was a great cook and regularly expressed her love through sumptuous meals and comfort foods. Although she did not actually reside "over the valley and through the woods", her home was definitely the place to be on all food-oriented holidays, including birthdays (cake!), Christmas (cookies!), and of course, the ultimate All-American food holiday, Thanksgiving (turkey!). Like many Americans on this day, my family gorged ourselves with all that Nana placed on her over-loaded dining room table – mashed potatoes, stuffing, butternut squash, warm rolls, salads, corn casserole, and of course, the mandatory roasted turkey. Following this annual feast, my sister and I would fall into food-induced stupors, sleeping off our over-indulgence for several hours before rousting ourselves to eat one more piece of pie.

The Turkey (Tryptophan) Coma: A number of years later I learned that my post-feast drowsiness was (presumed to be) caused by to a specific nutrient in turkey, the amino acid trypto-phan. This theory, first put forth by a nutritionist, proposed that turkey meat contains unusually high levels of tryptophan. Once absorbed, tryptophan is used by the body to produce serotonin (a neurotransmitter) and melatonin (a hormone). The neurological pathway through which serotonin works has anti-anxiety and calming effects and melatonin helps to induce feelings of drowsiness (i.e. enhances sleep). Therefore, the theory goes, af-ter consuming a high-protein meal, in particular one that is high in tryptophan, the body's production of melatonin and serotonin increase, which in turn cause drowsiness, reduced anxiety and a calm state of mind. Presto – the post-turkey coma!

The tryptophan/turkey theory became so popular and widespread in the early 1980's that nutrient supplement companies decided to by-pass the turkey part of the equation altogether and began producing and selling tryptophan supplements (L-tryptophan). These were initially promoted as sleep aids and to reduce signs of anxiety. However, as is the nature of these things, the promoted benefits of L-tryptophan rapidly expanded to include, among other things, claims that it would enhance athletic performance, cure facial pain, prevent premenstrual syndrome, and enhance attention in children with attention deficit-hyperactivity disorder. (My personal favorite was the promotion of L-tryptophan as a treatment for Tourette's syndrome). L-tryptophan enjoyed a robust reputation as the nutrient for "all that ails ye'" until 1989, when it was found to be responsible for causing eosinophilia-myalgia in more than 5000 people, killing at least 37 and permanently disabling hundreds. The US Food and Drug Administration quickly banned its import and sale as a supplement. Although the problem was eventually traced to a contaminant in a supplement that was imported from a Japanese supply company (and not the L-tryptophan itself), the ban remained in effect until 2009. Today, L-tryptophan is once again available as a nutrient supplement but it has never regained its earlier popularity in the human supplements world.

Tryptophan and Dogs: Given its history, it is odd that L-tryptophan was largely ignored by the dog world until a research paper published in 2000 suggested that feeding supplemental L-tryptophan might reduce dominance-related or territorial aggression in dogs (1).The researchers also studied dogs with problem excitability and hyperactivity, but found no effect of L-tryptophan on either of these behaviors. However, the paper led to the belief that tryptophan supplementation was an effective calming aid in dogs (which it definitely did not show in the study) and as an aid in reducing problem aggression. Today, a range of L-tryptophan supplements are marketed for reducing anxiety and inducing calmness in dogs. Interestingly, none are pure L-tryptophan, but rather also include other agents that are purported to have a calming effect on dogs, such as chamomile flower, passion flower, valerian root, or ginger.

So, what does the science say? Does eating turkey or taking an L-tryptophan supplement reduce anxiety and induce calmness? And, can it be used as an effective nutrient supplement to reduce anxiety-related problem behaviors in dogs?

The Turkey Myth: It is a myth that consuming turkey induces exceptional drowsiness or reduces anxiety. The theory fails on several counts. First, turkey meat does not actually contain a uniquely high level of tryptophan. The amount of tryptophan it contains is similar to that found in other meats and is only *half* of the concentration found in some plant-source proteins, such as soy. (Do you get sleepy after gorging on tofu?). Second, researchers have shown that the amount of tryptophan that is consumed after a normal high-protein meal, even one that contains a lot of tryptophan, does not come close to being high enough to cause significant changes in serotonin levels in the blood or in the synapses of neurons, where it matters the most. Third, to be converted into serotonin (and eventually into melatonin) tryptophan that is carried in the bloodstream following a meal must cross the blood-brain barrier and enter the brain. This barrier is quite selective and only accepts a certain number of amino acids of each type. Tryptophan is a very large molecule and competes with several other similar types of amino acids to make it across the barrier. Following a meal, especially if the meal is high in protein, tryptophan does increase in the blood and is pounding at the blood-barrier door for access. However, it is also competing with other amino acids that are also at high levels (turkey contains all of 'em). As a result, very limited amounts of tryptophan make it into the brain for conversion following a meal that includes lots of other nutrients.

So, why so sleepy? The real explanation for the drowsiness and euphoria that we all feel following a great turkey dinner at Nana's house is more likely to be caused by simply eating too much (which leads to reduced blood flow and oxygen to the brain as your body diverts resources to the mighty job at hand of digestion), imbibing in a bit of holiday (alcoholic) cheer, and possibly, eating a lot of high-carbohydrate foods such as potatoes, yams, and breads, which lead to a relatively wider fluctuation in circulating insulin levels. Whatever the cause, don't blame the turkey or the tryptophan.

Tryptophan Flying Solo: The erroneous focus upon turkey did have some positive consequences in that it lead to a closer look at tryptophan's potential impact upon mental states and behavior when provided as a supplement. As a serotonin precursor, tryptophan (and its metabolite 5-hydroxytryptophan or 5-HTP) has been studied as either a replacement or an adjunct therapy for serotonin reuptake inhibitors (SRRIs), medications that are commonly used to treat depression in people and are sometimes prescribed as treatment for anxiety-related behaviors in dogs. Although limited work has been conducted regarding the effects of tryptophan supplementation in dogs, several informative papers did follow the initial dog study of 2000:

Study 1: Tryptophan and Anxiety: Researchers at Wageningen University in the Netherlands studied a group of 138 privately-owned dogs with anxiety-related behavior problems (2). *Study design:* Half of the dogs were fed a standard dog food (control) and half were fed the same food, formulated to contain supplemental L-tryptophan. Neither the owners nor the researchers were privy to dogs' assigned groups. In other words, this was a "double-blind, placebo-controlled study", the "Gold Standard" of research designs. Dogs were fed their assigned diet for 8 weeks, during which time the owners recorded behavior changes. At the end of the study, the researchers also performed a set of behavior evaluations to assess the dogs. *Results:* Although blood tryptophan levels increased significantly (by 37 %) in the dogs that were fed supplemental tryptophan, neither the owners nor the researchers observed any difference in behavior between the supplemented group of dogs and the control dogs. There were moderate changes in behavior over time in *all* of the dogs, but this change was attributed to a placebo effect (more about placebos in next month's column). *Overall, supplementation with L-tryptophan demonstrated no anxiety-reducing effects in the dogs enrolled in this study.*

Study 2: Tryptophan and Abnormal-repetitive Behaviors: This was another double-blind and placebo-controlled study (3). In addition, the researchers used a "cross-over" design in which half of the dogs are first fed the control and the other half are first fed the test diet for a period of time and are then all switched to the alternate diet for a second study period. This is a well-accepted study design that is helpful when a researcher has limited number of subjects and that helps to control for the placebo effect. A group of 29 dogs was identified, each presenting with a form of abnormal-repetitive behavior. These were: circling, anxiety-related lick granuloma, light chasing/shadow staring, or stool eating. (Note: One might question the inclusion of stool-eating in this study, since many pet professionals consider eating feces to be a form of scavenging behavior that is normal and common in the domestic dog). Dogs were treated for 2-week periods and the frequencies of their abnormal behaviors were recorded daily. *Results:* The researchers reported no effect of supplemental L-tryptophan on the frequency or intensity of abnormal-repetitive behaviors. Although the owners reported slight improvements over time, this occurred both when dogs were receiving the supplemental tryptophan and while they were eating the control diet (there is the insidious placebo effect again). Limitations of this study were that it was very short-term and it targeted uncommon behavior problems that are notoriously resistant to treatment. *Still, this study did not provide any evidence to support a use of tryptophan supplementation for repetitive behavior problems in dogs. (So, to all you folks who live with poop-eaters - sorry, no easy answer here with L-tryptophan).*

Study 3: Tryptophan-enhanced Diet and Anxiety: Dogs with anxiety-related behavior problems were fed either a control food or the same food supplemented with L-tryptophan plus alpha-casozepine, a small peptide that originates from milk protein (4). This was a *single-blind*, cross-over study in which only dog owners were blinded to treatments. All of the dogs were first fed the control diet for 8 weeks and were all then switched to the test diet for a second 8-week period. Because the treatment group always followed the control in this study design, it is impossible to distinguish between a placebo effect and an actual diet effect in this study. (Note: This is a serious research design flaw that the study authors mention only briefly). *Results:* A small reduction in owner-scored anxiety-related behaviors was found for four of the five identified anxiety problems. However, in all of the cases, initial severity of the problems were rated as very low (~1 to 1.5 on a five-point scale in which a score of 0 denoted an absence of the problem and a score of 5 denoted its highest severity), and the change in score was numerically very small, though statistically significant. This is not surprising since there is not very much wiggle room between a score of 1 and a score of 0. Finally, given that the food was supplemented with both L-tryptophan and casozepine, conclusions cannot be made specifically about L-tryptophan.

Take Away for Dog Folks: First, forget the turkey. While it can be a high-quality meat to feed to dogs (especially if you are selecting a food that includes human-grade meats or are cooking fresh for your dog), as a protein source turkey contains no more tryptophan than any other dietary protein. Feeding turkey to your dog will not promote calmness (unless of course, you allow him to stuff himself silly along with the rest of the family on Thanksgiving Day). Second, keep your skeptic cap firmly in place when considering the effectiveness of supplemental L-tryptophan or a tryptophan-enriched food as a treatment for anxiety-related problems. The early study in 2000 reported a modest effect in dogs with dominance-related aggression or territorial behaviors but found no effect in treating hyperactivity.

Subsequently, two placebo-controlled studies reported no effect at all and the single study that reported a small degree of behavior change could not discount the possibility of a placebo effect.

Human nature encourages us to gravitate toward easy fixes for things that ail our dogs. Hearing about a nutrient supplement or a specially-formulated food that proclaims to reduce anxiety and calm fearful dogs is powerful stuff for dog owners who are desperate to help their dogs. These types of claims are especially appealing because anxiety problems can have a terrible impact on a dog's quality of life and are often challenging to treat using standard (and proven) approaches to behavior modification. An additional risk that must be mentioned regarding our inclination to gravitate toward unverified nutritional "cures" is that well-established approaches such as behavior modification may be postponed or rejected by an owner who instead opts for the supplement, wasting precious time that could actually help a dog in need. Until we have stronger scientific evidence that demonstrates a role for L-tryptophan in changing problem behavior in our dogs, my recommendation is to enjoy the turkey, but train the dog.

CITED STUDIES:

1. DeNapoli JS, Dodman NH, Shuster L, et al. Effect of dietary protein content and tryptophan supplementation on dominance aggression, territorial aggression, and hyperactivity in dogs. *Journal of the American Veterinary Medical Association* 2000; 217:504-508.

2. Bosch G, Beerda B, Beynen AC, et al. Dietary tryptophan supplementation in privately owned mildly anxious dogs. *Applied Animal Behaviour Science* 2009; 121:197-205.

3. Kaulfuss P, Hintze S, Wurbel H. Effect of tryptophan as a dietary supplement on dogs with abnormal-repetitive behaviours. Abstract. *Journal of Veterinary Behavior* 2009; 4:97.

4. Kato M, Miyaji K, Ohtani N, Ohta M. Effects of prescription diet on dealing with stressful situations and performance of anxiety-related behaviors in privately owned anxious dogs. *Journal of Veterinary Behavior* 2012; 7:21-26.

14
This Test that You Keep Using......

(I do not think that it means what you think it means......)

The *availability heuristic* is a common cognitive error that influences our ability to make accurate decisions. It is operating full-force whenever we base a decision upon evidence that is easily available (i.e. dramatic, obvious, easily measured) but that may not actually reflect reality. In practice, this means that we pay more attention to evidence that is salient (obvious and dramatic) and tend to ignore evidence that may be more compelling but not quite so sensational.

Take for example, shark attacks. The feeling that shark attacks are far more common and that we are at greatly inflated risk than we actually are occurs because of the extensive and sensationalist media coverage that a single shark encounter attracts. As a result, when you consider going to the beach this summer, an image of a shark pops into your mind because such an image is highly available to you. However, while shark attacks can and do happen, an examination of the actual risk is much lower that our perceptions lead us to believe. Here are the facts about shark attacks:

- Number of people killed by coconuts last year: **150**
- Number of people killed by sharks last year: **10**

Therefore, you are in greater danger of dying from getting knocked on the head by a falling coconut than you are from getting killed by shark.

So.....What does this have to do with Dogs? I will return to the significance of the availability heuristic shortly. (There will be a tie-in, I promise). Let's now turn to an important dog topic - the

89

expression of food-related aggression in dogs. Food-related aggression (FA) in dogs is specific subtype of resource guarding in dogs. Its expression can vary in intensity from a dog who simply shows tenseness near his food bowl, to freezing, growling, or biting a person who interferes with the dog while he or she is eating. Most of the standardized behavior evaluations that are used by shelters and rescue groups include an assessment for FA. For reasons of safety, many use a fake plastic or rubber hand that is attached to a long stick for this test. Although procedures vary somewhat, the test for FA involves interfering with the dog while he is eating from a bowl, first by placing the fake hand into the bowl and pulling it away and then by attempting to push the dog's face away from his food by pressing the instrument alongside the dog's face. The validity of this test, meaning its ability to correctly identify dogs who do (and do not) truly have FA, is an important issue because dogs who exhibit FA during a behavior evaluation are almost always identified as an adoption risk, which can lead to reduced opportunities for finding a home, and at some shelters, to automatic euthanasia.

2004 Study: Despite its ubiquitous inclusion in behavior tests, few studies have actually examined the reliability of the fake hand test for FA. A few years ago, a group of researchers at Cornell conducted a study with dogs who had a history of various forms of aggression, including FA (1). They found a positive and statistically significant correlation between showing an aggressive response toward the fake hand and previously exhibited aggression in the dog. However, the relationship was weak and a substantial number of dogs who were NOT aggressive in "real life" were found to react aggressively toward the fake hand when tested. The authors recommended the use of caution when using a fake hand in behavior tests because of the high number of both false positive (dogs aggressing to the fake hand who did not show FA in their homes) and false negative responses (dogs who did not react to the fake hand but did show FA in their homes) that they found. A limitation of this study was that because the researchers used dogs with a known history of different types of aggression who were already in their permanent homes, they could not make conclusions about the *predictive* value of the test. To do this, we needed a study that examined how well the fake hand test, when administered to dogs in a shelter environment, correlates with dogs' *future* behavior when living in homes. Such a study was published in September, 2013 in the journal *Applied Animal Behaviour Science* (2).

2013 Study: Dr. Amy Marder and her colleagues at the Center for Shelter Dogs located in Boston, MA tested a group of 97 dogs using a standardized canine behavior evaluation that included a fake hand test for FA. Dogs showing extreme aggression or multiple forms of aggression were excluded from the study for ethical and safety reasons. Following testing, all of the dogs were adopted into homes. Adopters of dogs who showed food aggression (FA+) were provided with additional instructions for handling the dog during feeding times, but the dogs themselves received no additional training or behavior modification prior to adoption. Adoptive owners were surveyed to assess the dog's behavior in the home at 3 days, 3 weeks and 3 months following adoption.

Results: Of the group of 97 tested dogs, 20 dogs (21 %) reacted aggressively to the hand and were classified as FA-positive (FA+); 77 dogs (79 %) did not react and were identified as FA-negative (FA-). Of the 20 dogs who were classified as FA+, approximately half (11/20, 55 %) were reported by their owners to show food-related aggression while in the home. However, nine of the FA+ dogs (45 %) showed no signs of food aggression when in their adoptive home. Of the 77 dogs who were classified as FA-, the majority (60/77, 78 %) were FA- when in their adoptive homes. However, 17 dogs from this group, 22 percent, did show signs of FA when in the home, even though they had tested negative for FA while in the shelter and tested with the fake hand. A final result was that the majority of owners of dogs who were showing FA in the home reported that they did not consider their dog's behavior to be problematic and that they would definitely adopt the same dog again.

Take Away for Dog Folks: The authors found that the *negative predictive value* of the test was **high** since 78 percent of dogs who tested negative in a shelter environment showed no food aggressive behaviors when in their adoptive home. (**This is good**). Conversely, the *positive predictive value* of the test was **low** since only 55 percent of dogs who tested positive in the shelter environment actually showed food aggression when in the home (**This is bad**). In addition, and perhaps as important, owners may perceive food-related aggression as *much less problematic than do shelter staff* and may have little trouble managing dogs who are reactive around their food bowls.

If that information does not give you enough to chew upon, let me contribute an additional question to this controversial (and apparently quite polarized) topic. *What do these data say about the test itself?* There is really no question that the data presented in this study, along with the earlier Cornell study, suggest something additional. Realizing that this is a sacred cow to those who are highly committed to their fake hands, I offer up the suggestion that *perhaps the fake-hand test is not measuring what its users think it is measuring. (In other words, it is not a valid test of FA).*

Here is Why (stay with me here; this gets long but it is worth the ride.....): The researchers reported positive and negative predictive values for the fake hand test (numbers noted above), but they also had data available to calculate two additional measures of a diagnostic test's validity. These are referred to as *sensitivity* (a test's ability to correctly identify all positive responses) and *specificity* (its ability to correctly identify all negative responses). I went ahead and punched these numbers using the data that the paper provided and found this:

- **Fake Hand Test Sensitivity = 39 percent.** This means that 39 percent of the time, the fake-hand correctly identified FA in the dogs who actually had it. The flip side of this statistic is probably more important. It also means that almost 2/3 of the time (61 %), the fake-hand either incorrectly identified a dog who was FA- as being FA+ or missed the identification and labeled a dog who was FA+ as being FA-. Although sensitivity values are considered to be a relative measure, I do not think anyone would try to argue that 39 percent success rate signifies a valid test. (Especially in light of the fact that a positive result for this particular test can mean the end of life for the dog).

- **Fake Hand Test Specificity = 87 percent.** This means that the majority of the time, if the fake hand says a dog is non-reactive around his food bowl, it is correct. Only 13 percent of dogs who tested FA- actually had FA. While this is a desirable value for the test, high specificity alone is simply not enough.

- **Supporting data?** This was not the first study that has examined the use of the fake hand in behavior evaluations, but it is the first study that has measured the predictive value of the test. It is important to note that to date, there are no published studies that provide data showing that using a fake hand to diagnose food reactivity in dogs is a highly reliable test. None.

Knowing this, one might logically ask - *Why do temperament tests that are used with shelter dogs continue to include the fake hand as a test for food aggression?*

There are a few possibilities:

1. **It is simple and measurable:** Unlike much of what we do in behavior and training, the Fake Hand test is pretty easy to administer and to score. Therefore, it is a shoe-in for being

included in a battery of tests that can be quickly administered to a lot of dogs and by personnel who have varying levels of expertise.

2. **The use of the fake hand is well-established:** Many, but not all, of the behavior assessment tests that are used in shelters today include a test for FA that uses a fake hand (3,4). Many of these tests are highly standardized and include specific training programs for shelter staff who administer them. However, while proponents of the fake hand insist that a set of clear and very specific steps are used in the test's administration (i.e. how far to stand away from the bowl, how many times the dog's face is pushed, how to manipulate the bowl), such protestations are a moot point since none of the specific guidelines for administering the tests have been validated either.

3. **The results are dramatic and salient - i.e. AVAILABLE:** (Here is the tie-in). A dog who reacts aggressively when a fake hand is shoved in his face while he is eating provides us with an example of the availability heuristic in action. Aggressive responses in dogs elicit dramatic and involuntary reactions in those who witness the response - a rush of adrenaline, a bit of fear, perhaps even a little bit of the "stopping to watch a car wreck" feeling, if you will. Just as we react strongly (and illogically) to reports of shark attacks, so too might an evaluator react emotionally to an aggressing dog. The fallout is that the aggression that is provoked by a fake hand during a behavior test may acquire more significance than it actually has in real life. (This is supported by Dr. Marder's results when interviewing owners of FA+ dogs, who did not see FA as being such a big deal). And, because the provoked aggressive response in the dog is dramatic and obvious, the evaluator now feels compelled to do something about the reaction that was provoked - special adopts, no adopt, euthanize.

Up on my Soapbox

Here's a bombshell: *Perhaps poking a dog in the face with a fake hand while he is eating in a shelter environment is not a valid way to test for food aggression:* The sensitivity statistic of 39 percent suggests that at least some (if not the majority) of dogs who react when tested with a fake hand are not showing FA. At the very least, this paper and this particular statistic suggests that the presumed test for FA using a fake hand is not testing for the thing that proponents think it is testing for. Additionally, the availability error may lead those who regularly administer this test to assign excessive significance to FA because of the salience of provoked responses in the test and highly inflated perceptions of risk to owners. Given that the fake hand test leads to decisions that severely reduce a dog's chances of being adopted into a home or may even result in the death of the dog, this is a possibility that must be raised and considered.

CITED STUDIES:

1. Kroll TL, Houpt KA, Erb HN. The use of novel stimuli as indicators of aggressive behavior in dogs. *Journal of the American Animal Hospital Association* 2004; 40:13-19.

2. Marder AR, Shabelansky A, Patronek GJ, Dowling-Guyer S, D'Arpino SS. Food-related aggression in shelter dogs: A comparison of behavior identified by a behavior evaluation in the shelter and owner reports after adoption. *Applied Animal Behaviour Science* 2013; 148:150-156.

3. Barnard S, Siracusa C, Reisner I, et al. Validity of model devices used to assess canine temperament in behavioral tests. *Applied Animal Behaviour Science* 2012; 138:79-87.

4. Taylor KD, Mills DS. The development and assessment of temperament tests for adult companion dogs. *Journal of Veterinary Behavior* 2006; 1:94-108.

15
Beware the Straw Man

What does the research tell us about the effectiveness of standardized behavior tests with shelter dogs?

Many animal shelters regularly use standardized tests to assess the behavior of dogs and to determine adoption suitability. However, while the use of these tests has become ubiquitous, there is a distinct lack of research demonstrating their reliability or validity. In other words, while testing a dog's degree of friendliness, aggression and fear prior to adoption makes intuitive sense and *feels* like a good idea, we do not actually know whether or not it actually works. This is an important question to raise (and I am by no means the first to be raising it), because when these tests are administered as a method for predicting a dog's future behavior, the dog's performance on the test often determines whether or not he *has* a future.

The previous essay, "*This Test that You Keep Using.....*" reviewed a study that examined the predictive value of a single subtest of a standard behavior test, the fake hand as a test for food aggression (1). That paper's results are important because it brought the fake hand test under scientific scrutiny and attracted attention to the need for the scientific validation of all behavior tests that are used with shelter and rescue dogs.

Though still limited, these studies are being conducted and published. For example, an Australian behaviorist, Kate Mornement, has been studying behavior assessments used by animal shelters for the last several years as part of her PhD research at Monash University (2,3). Most recently, she examined the effectiveness of a behavior assessment program called the BARK protocol (4).

The Study: Kate and her research team first worked with a focus panel of nine canine experts to develop a standardized 12-subtest behavior assessment that was labeled the Behavioural Assessment for Rehoming K-9s (BARK) program. The BARK battery of tests was designed to assess five primary behavior traits: anxiety, compliance, fear, friendliness, and activity level. Following development, the BARK test's reliability and validity were studied in a shelter setting over a 12-month period. Several measures of its effectiveness were examined: *inter-rater reliability* (the degree to which different evaluators agreed when assessing the same dog), *test-retest* (the degree to which a dog's score was stable over time; in this case dogs were retested 24 hours following their initial assessment), and, of high importance for shelter dogs, *predictive validity* (the accuracy with which in-shelter test results predicted a dog's in-home behavior). Predictive validity was assessed by surveying adoptive owners several months following adoption regarding their dog's degree of anxiety, fear, friendliness, compliance, and activity level.

Results: Several results of this study are of value to shelter professionals, dog trainers and dog owners:

1. **Inter-rater reliability:** Scoring for the five behavior categories showed statistically significant and moderate agreement between evaluators when testing the same dog. This means that two evaluators (who in this study were experienced researchers) generally rated dogs similarly. Some associations were stronger than others, with the assessment for fearful behavior showing the strongest correlation (agreement) between scorers.

2. **Test-retest reliability:** The test-retest reliability was significant for some traits and non-significant for others, resulting in overall weak reliability for the entire group of subtests. This means that a dog's scores were not always consistent (stable) over time (in this case, just 24 hours!) while living in

the shelter environment. Similar to inter-rater reliability scoring, the tests that reflected a dog's degree of fear had the strongest correlations. This means that a dog who tested fearfully on the first day tended to continue to test fearfully on the following day. However, scores for other traits were not as consistent over time.

3. **Predictive validity:** A group of 67 dogs who had been adopted into homes were subsequently assessed via owner interviews. Owner assessments were compared with the dogs' in-shelter BARK scores. Overall, the predictive value of the BARK test was found to be poor. Only two of the five behavior categories had statistically significant correlations between in-home behavior and BARK test scores; fear and friendliness. However, even these associations were not strong ($r = 0.42$ and $r = 0.49$, respectively). There were no correlations between in-home reports of anxiety, compliance, and activity level with in-shelter BARK scores. These results are perhaps the most important, since they tell us that the test was not accurately predicting how a dog would or would not behave once he or she was adopted into their new home (which, not to put too sharp a point on it, is supposed to be the entire purpose of these tests in the first place).

Take Away for Dog Folks: These results suggest that a standardized behavior test, administered to shelter dogs in a shelter environment, may not be a reliable indicator of a dog's future behavior. In my personal opinion, this study, coupled with the study of the fake hand test, have some pretty important implications for dogs.

Up on my Soapbox

Soapbox Time: These results (and those of Marder et al.) raise several questions. Perhaps single-session tests designed to measure major behavior categories can work and all that is needed is additional attention to designing the right types of subtests. Or, perhaps it is more important to examine differences among shelters in terms of staff experience, time availability, adoption standards, and the number of animals that are cared for and attempt to design behavior assessments that can be modified to fit individual shelter's needs. *Or, perhaps it is time to rethink the entire use of these tests and to consider not using them at all.*

Bring out the Straw Man: Because these tests have become so entrenched in shelter and rescue dog culture, it is this last suggestion that is not only often overlooked, but also that has the potential to raise much ire. Typically, test proponents' responses to this suggestion center around three objections, all of which qualify in one way or another as *straw man arguments.*

Straw man arguments are a well-established type of rhetoric that involve first misrepresenting an opponent's position (usually, as we will see, to ridiculous lengths), and then refuting that position (which is not difficult, seeing that the opponent's arguments were distorted in the first place). As a result "attacking a straw man" creates the *illusion* of having effectively refuted or defeated an opponent's proposition when in fact, all that has happened is that thoughtful discourse has been diverted or derailed altogether. (Not surprisingly, many politicians and their handlers are masters at engaging in Straw Man arguments).

These three Straw Men are commonly used whenever a beloved behavior evaluation test is questioned (each argument is followed by an explanation of its fallacy):

1. **If we stopped using the [insert branded test name here] behavior test, we would not have a way to assess dogs' behavior prior to putting them up for adoption.** *Setting up a false dichotomy:* It is not an either/or issue. There are other, potentially better, approaches to monitoring and assessing shelter dog behavior than single-session standardized tests. Not using the [***] test, does *not* require you to use nothing at all to assess behavior.

2. **I have seen the tests work with my own eyes; if it prevents a single dog who is aggressive from going up for adoption from my shelter, it is worth using.** *False proposition:* Marder's data show that yes, some dogs are correctly identified as food aggressive. However, others are missed, and some dogs who are not aggressive are misidentified as such. A poor diagnostic test that gets one right once in a while cannot be defended as a valid diagnostic test.

3. **But, what about the children? We cannot risk adopting out a dog who might bite a child!!?! (This last is typically uttered at a high octave and carrying a hint of hysteria)** *Classic Straw Man:* Redefining the argument to imply that those who question the use of the beloved test advocate the release of baby-killing canines into communities. This is misdirection at its best as invoking the emotional "save the children" chant works to derail discourse every time. First, no one denies that it is important to ensure that only dogs who are safe are placed into homes with children. Second, the fact that it is important to identify dogs who may be aggressive to children is not the same issue as whether or not one continues to use tests that appear to be unreliable. (In other words, an inaccurate test would not help you to save those children that you are so concerned about.....)

Beware the Straw Man: Straw man arguments, in addition to being logically invalid, function to keep people from paying attention to the evidence, and from admitting that there may be a problem with the use of behavior tests to assess shelter dogs. If we can keep these at bay and instead encourage discussion of where the science seems to be leading us, we may find that there are potential alternatives to the current standardized, single-session behavior tests. Improved design of the tests is one, as is custom-designing tests to meet shelters' needs, as is developing an approach that is more longitudinal in nature - for example, having shelter staff note simple behaviors once or twice a day during feeding/cleaning/exercising dogs to provide a longer-term and cumulative record of a dog's behavior. Longitudinal data, like single-session behavior tests, would require validation through scientific testing. Conversely, to continue to champion a battery of tests that have not yet held up under scientific scrutiny and *have* been shown to be significantly deficient in at least some areas, seems to be helping no one, least of all the dogs who are tested........and fail.

CITED STUDIES:

1. Marder AR, Shabelansky A, Patronek GJ, Dowling-Guyer S, D'Arpino SS. Food-related aggression in shelter dogs: A comparison of behavior identified by a behavior evaluation in the shelter and owner reports after adoption. Applied Animal Behaviour Science 2013; 148:150-156.

2. Mornement K, Toukhsati S, Coleman G, et al. Reliability, validity and feasibility of existing tests of canine behavior. AIAM Annual Conference on Urban Animal Management, Proceedings. 2009;11-18.

3. Mornement KM, Coleman GJ, Toukhsati S, Bennett PC. A review of behavioural assessment protocols used by Australian animal shelters to determine adoption suitability of dogs. Journal of Applied Animal Welfare Science 2010; 13:314-329.

4. Mornement KM, Coleman GJ, Toukhsati S, Bennett PC. Development of the behavioural assessment for re-homing K9's (B.A.R.K.) protocol. Applied Animal Behaviour Science 2013; 151:75-83.

Part 3 – Training

16
Treat Please!

Food treats, petting & praise are studied as positive reinforcers during training. Which do dogs respond to best?

One of the things that I love best about training dogs (and there are many things to love about training dogs) is that they respond well to so many different types of positive reinforcement. We have a wide variety of "fun stuff" from which to choose to send the message to our dogs that says: "*Yes!!! That is it!! You are SO very, very smart and good!!*" We can use food treats, petting, verbal praise, an opportunity to play tug, a retrieving game, or even a chance to play with a best dog buddy.

Food as a Primary Reinforcer: Food is generally considered to be one of the most, if not *the* most, powerful and universal primary reinforcer that we use in dog training. A primary reinforcer refers to a stimulus that needs no prior conditioning or learning – it is imbued, if you will, with traits that make it inherently pleasing and desirable to our dogs. As a training aid, this is true simply because most dogs love to eat, (and as far as I can tell anyway, all dogs gotta eat). Social interactions such as verbal praise, petting, and playing are also effective positive reinforcers, but dogs seem to vary considerably in their responses to these. Some turn inside out for cuddle time while others do better with a rousing game of tug-o-war. The cool thing is that we have a wide range of things - food treats, various ways to convey love and affection, and all sorts of play to use as positive reinforcers that help our dogs to learn. Still, there continue to be trainers and owners who reject the use of food treats and insist that dogs respond equally well to praise and petting as they do to food treats. In a recent study, Megumi Fukuzawa and Naomi Hayashi of Nihon University in Japan asked exactly this question (1).

105

The Study: The researchers randomly assigned a group of 15 adult dogs to one of three treatment groups. All groups were trained first to do a short sit/stay exercise (baseline training) and then to "come when called" from increasingly long distances. All of the dogs were trained by a single trainer and each group differed only in the type of positive reinforcement (+R) that was used. These were either food (soft moist dog treats), stroking (gentle petting on the head and shoulders), or praise ("good boy/girl!").

Results: First, all of the dogs learned the tasks successfully. However, the number of sessions to attain proficiency and the response times differed with the type of reinforcer that was used:

1. **Sit stay:** When food treats were used to positively reinforce sit and stay, the number of sessions needed to learn the task was significantly fewer than when praise or petting was used (4.8 sessions for food; 12.8 and 12.4 sessions for praise and stroking, respectively).

2. **Come when called:** When food was used to teach come when called, the response time was significantly faster than when either stroking or praise were used as positive reinforcers. Praise fared slightly better than petting for this exercise, but the difference was not statistically significant.

3. **And.....**Interestingly, when the trainer was closest to the dogs during the early "come when called" sessions, the dogs responded almost equally well to all three reinforcers, with food showing a slight but non-significant advantage.

Take Away for Dog Folks: This study supports what so many trainers know and use daily: Food treats, petting and praise are *all* effective positive reinforcers with dogs. Using food treats may enhance learning by reducing the number of sessions needed to acquire proficiency and speeds response time. So keep those treats in your bag of tricks - They work well and your dog loves you for it!

CITED STUDY:

Fukuzawa M and Hayashi N: Comparison of 3 different reinforcements of learning in dogs (Canis familiaris). *Journal of Veterinary Behavior* 2013; 8:221-224.

17
Speaking of Treats

Do dogs "rate" their food treats and respond differently to high-value versus low value treats during training?

Many trainers selectively use what we call "high-value treats" for some behaviors and "low-value treats" for others. However, other than subjectively observing the level of a dog's pleasure at receiving different types of treats, do we have actual evidence that treats vary in their influence upon learning? For example, does my Toller, Chip learn faster or more efficiently when I use homemade tuna treats versus small, dry biscuits? Intuitively, I think that he does, since he almost climbs into the oven when he smells his treats baking (the only thing I am even remotely capable of producing in the kitchen, by the way).

Lucky for us, some scientists have already asked this question and are providing some answers.

The Study: Mariana Bentosela and her co-investigators trained a group of 13 adult (pet) dogs to offer eye contact using either a high incentive treat (dried liver pieces), or a low incentive treat (dry kibble pieces) as the positive reinforcer. The methods used to train this behavior are the same as those used in the study that I reviewed previously in *"Treat Please"*. In this study, all of the dogs rapidly learned "gazing behavior" using both types of reinforcer and all readily consumed the treats that were provided, regardless of the type. Following the initial learning phase of the experiment, the dogs were rested for one hour and a second training session was conducted.

In the second session, training was exactly the same, except that all of the dogs now received dry dog food pieces as their reinforcers. The investigators refer to this as "down-shifting" the dogs who had been previously trained using liver treats. (In this study, the dogs who were trained in both sessions with dry kibble are the control group). Behaviors that were measured included the number of trials to acquisition, gaze duration, food rejection, and general behavior and communication signals.

Results: The researchers were interested in finding out if dogs, like several other mammals, would react to a change from a high-value to a low-value reinforcer when the behavior was initially taught using the high-value treat. Here is what they found:

- **High value treats:** During the initial training phase, although all of the dogs learned to offer gaze, dogs trained using the high-value treat maintained eye contact for a significantly longer duration than did dogs trained using the low-value treat (23.1 vs. 15.7 seconds, respectively).

- **Down-shifting:** During the second phase, dogs who were downshifted from liver to kibble rapidly decreased their gaze duration, while the control dogs who had been offered kibble in both trials showed an increase in gaze duration. (This second result was unexpected).

- **Treat rejections**: Dogs who had been trained with liver and then switched to kibble rejected the food on significantly more occasions when offered kibble than did dogs who were trained consistently with the kibble pieces. Most commonly, the dog would approach the treat being offered, sniff the treat in the trainer's hand, and then walk away without eating it.

Take Away for Dog Folks: First, we must note that the study groups used in this experiment were quite small (6 dogs in the control group and 7 dogs in the experimental group), and that the behavior that was trained is very simple and is easily accomplished by most dogs. However, even with these limitations, the results suggest that learning is influenced by the value of the positive reinforcer that is used and that dogs are affected by changes in *anticipated* reinforcer value. Dogs trained with high-value treats showed a stronger response (longer duration of gaze), but also demonstrated signs of extinction when suddenly switched to a low-value treat, even rejecting the reinforcer!

Most trainers who pay attention to different value reinforcers use high-value treats when training a difficult or complex behavior. Typically, we pair high-value treats with the behavior that is most difficult or the part of a sequence that the dog is least motivated to offer. (If back-chaining, the last behavior gets the highest value treat). The results of this study tell us that, yes, using a variety of treat types can be helpful, and that yes, high value treats may enhance learning. However, the results also suggest that we might want to pay close attention to *downshifting from high to lower value treats during training sessions*. Dogs may not only notice the switch, but it can affect the stability of a previously trained behavior, at least when that behavior has been only recently learned and is not yet reliable.

So trainers - Continue to rank your treats and pay careful attention to the value that they have to your dog, both when you are using the high-value stuff *and* when you throw in that handful of dried kibble or biscuits now and then.

CITED STUDY:

Bentosela, M, Jakovcevic A, Elgier AM, Mustaca AE, Papini MR. Incentive contrast in domestic dogs (*Canis familiaris*). *Journal of Comparative Psychology* 2009; 123:125-130.

18
Yogi Bear Dogs

Two studies tease out the effects of positive-based training methods on dogs' ability to learn new tasks.

Do you live with a Yogi Bear dog? You know what I mean - one of those smarter than the average bear dogs? I am quite certain that I live with several. For example, Chip, my Toller, excels at retrieving rings and carefully placing them over a pylon, riding a skateboard (sometimes recklessly, in my opinion), and playing a game of his own invention called Agility Ring-Toss. Our ever resourceful Brittany, Vinny, demonstrates his version of canine genius by finding a hidden object after seeing it for less than a second, and our youngster, Cooper, shows himself to be a Puppy Einstein each time that he learns a new trick, typically before I have a chance to complete my prescribed schedule of shaping. And Cadie, now 14-years-young, demonstrated her canine intellect by learning not only to fake a hurt paw, but to limp pathetically on three legs and fall to the ground in a full-blown melodramatic swoon when she decided to ad lib her own version of this popular trick.

All of their antics? *Clicker trained.*

Clicker training is a popular and by all accounts highly successful training technique that requires the use of positive reinforcement, the "treat" part of click-treat. Many trainers, including me, are convinced that focusing on positive reinforcement during training promotes a *"love of learning"* in dogs. And, it follows, these dogs should be more likely to develop into individuals who are "smarter than the average bear". However, as we all know, anecdotal experiences (even lots of them) do not add up to scientific evidence. So, is there evidence that supports the belief that training, and specifically training that is reward-based, leads to smarter dogs? Let's look at two recent studies:

Study 1: The first was conducted by Sarah Marshall-Pescini and her colleagues at the University of Milan in Italy (1). They examined the success of two groups of dogs presented with a novel problem-solving task. The first group included pet dogs who had either no previous training at all or had completed a single basic obedience class early in life (untrained dogs; n = 54). The second group consisted of dogs who had been extensively trained in a variety of dog sports such as agility, search and rescue, retrieving sports or Schutzhund (trained dogs; n = 56). All of the dogs in the trained group had been trained using positive reinforcement (food treats and/or a toy as the reinforcer). During the study, each dog was individually tested for his/her ability to solve a box-opening task. They used a plastic container that was holding a dog treat and that could be opened either by the dog hitting a pad with a paw or using his/her nose to lift the lid. Other than watching their owner first open the box to show them the treat inside, the dogs received no aid during the problem-solving session. The experimenters measured several variables as the dogs worked at the problem. These included the dog's success/failure, the amount of time needed to open the box, and the type of behaviors that the dog exhibited while working out the problem.

Results: Significantly more dogs in the trained group were successful at opening the box than were dogs in the untrained group (34 vs 16 dogs, p = 0.0002). Trained dogs also spent more time interacting with the box and less time orienting to their owners when attempting to solve the problem. Interestingly, the type of training that the dogs had experienced had no effect upon their ability to solve the task. In other words, agility, Schutzhund, and SAR dogs were all equally proficient at solving the unique box-opening task.

Study 2: The second study was conducted by Nicola Rooney and her colleagues at the University of Bristol in the UK (2). Fifty-three dog owners first completed a detailed survey that asked a series of questions regarding their preferred method of dog training. Following completion of the survey, each owner was videotaped in their home while they interacted with their dog and while training their dog to respond to a new command. The experimenters measured degree of positive reinforcement (treats, praise, petting) versus negative reinforcement (harsh voice, collar corrections, swatting/hitting) that owners preferred and then analyzed each dogs' videotaped behavior for rate of learning and success, and type of behaviors exhibited during every day interactions with their owner. They also analyzed the dogs' behavior in the home when interacting with visitors.

Results: The study found that dogs owned by people who reported using a high proportion of punishment during training were less likely to interact with unfamiliar people visiting the home and were significantly less playful when compared with the dogs of owners who reported that they trained their dog using primarily positive methods. In addition, the dogs of owners who stated that they used reward-based training and who were classified via survey results as being highly patient with their dogs tended to perform better in the training task, but this difference was not statistically significant.

Take Away for Dog Folks: Each of these two studies has strengths and weaknesses, and together provide a nice bit of helpful information to trainers and dog owners. The first study is a rock star in terms of dog numbers; over 100 dogs studied in an applied dog study is a difficult and time-consuming feat - Bravo to the researchers for this! And, their results tell us that indeed, dogs who are regularly trained are more likely to engage in a novel problem-solving task, to work independently of their owner, and to be successful at solving the task. In other words, dogs who are trained regularly seem to have "*learned to learn*" (and may indeed be Yogi Bear dogs). What this study's results cannot tell us, however, is whether or not there is any difference in the performance of dogs who are trained using primarily positive reinforcement and those who are trained using more coercive methods. This limitation occurred because training methods that emphasized punishment or negative reinforcement were not examined in this study.

The second study, on the other hand, did compare dogs who were trained using primarily positive methods with those who were trained using more aversive (correction-based) methods. However, limitations of that study were that it utilized a self-reporting survey and that it did not measure dogs' problem-solving abilities. Keeping these in mind, the second study suggests that the use of coercive, punishment-based training methods with dogs may negatively influence a dog's behavior with other people and may inhibit rather than support learning. It also suggests that using methods that emphasize positive reinforcement may lead to more confident and playful dogs - something that most of us certainly desire.

CITED STUDIES:

1. Pescini-Marshall S, Valsecchi P, Petak I, et al. Does training make you smarter? The effect of training on dogs' performance (*Canis familiaris*) in a problem solving task. *Behavioural Processes* 2008; 78:449-454

2. Rooney NJ, Cowan S. Training methods and owner–dog interactions: Links with dog behaviour and learning ability. *Applied Animal Behaviour Science* 2011; 132:169-177.

19
Deconstructing the Click

A review of classical & operant conditioning and an examination of why clicker training works so well.

As I mentioned in the previous essay, I am a clicker trainer. All of my own dogs are clicker trained and many of the classes that we teach at my training school, AutumnGold, are "clicker-centric". Clicker training is not only a scientifically sound approach to teaching dogs new things, but is also a kind, enjoyable, and bond-strengthening method of training - something that benefits both dogs and their people.

What is clicker training? For the uninitiated, clicker training is a relatively simple technique that involves pairing the click sound made by a small, handheld clicker with the delivery of a food treat. (A clicker is a tiny, hand-held plastic box with an inner metal tongue that "clicks" when pushed). After several repetitions of this pairing (Click-Treat; hereafter CT), in which the click sound reliably predicts the treat, the sound comes to possess the same properties as the presentation of the treat itself - a pleasurable emotional response. Clicker training packs an enormously powerful positive punch for both the dog and the trainer because it allows the trainer to precisely target tiny bits of behavior at the exact moment they are occurring. The click sound becomes analogous to saying to your dog *"That's it!! That thing that you are doing right this instant is what will earn you the yummy treat that is coming shortly! You are SO very smart!"*

A second advantage of clicker training, a benefit that it shares with all training that emphasizes positive reinforcement, is that it shifts a substantial proportion of training control to the dog. This empowerment leads to a dog who loves to learn new things and is eager to *"find out what's clickin' in each training session"*. (Seriously there is nothing not to love about clicker training).

So let's deconstruct the click.

When I was teaching companion animal science at the University of Illinois, I spent a fair amount of time lecturing about two principle types of learning - classical conditioning and operant conditioning. Clicker training provides a great example of a training method that involves both forms of learning:

- **Classical conditioning** occurs when a subject responds to relationships between two or more stimuli. The basic elements of this type of learning are a *meaningless* stimulus (initially called a "neutral" stimulus) that elicits no response and a *meaningful* (unconditioned) stimulus that elicits a response without any prior conditioning. The consistent pairing of the two stimuli, with the neutral stimulus always preceding the unconditioned stimulus, results in a change in the meaning of the neutral stimulus. Because the neutral stimulus consistently *precedes and thus predicts* the unconditioned stimulus, it begins to elicit the same response that is elicited by the unconditioned stimulus (think Pavlov's dogs: A ringing bell, and then food). Generally speaking, many classically conditioned behaviors involve emotional responses such as pleasure/joy or fear, with the dog having little or no voluntary control over his/her response.

- **Operant conditioning** (also called instrumental learning) occurs as a result of the consequences of a (usually voluntary) behavior. This terminology originates from the concept that we are continually "operating on" our environment, and subsequently alter our behaviors in response to their good or bad consequences. Like other subjects, dogs tend to repeat behaviors that have desirable consequences. We say that these behaviors are positively reinforced (+R).

- **What's the difference?** Classical conditioning is concerned with establishing relationships between stimuli and functions as a primary way in which animals learn about their environment. Trainers think a lot about "predictors" in a dog's world and often will manage a dog's environment to reduce or eliminate stimuli that predict unpleasant experiences and try to increase stimuli that consistently predict pleasant experiences for the dog. Conversely, operant conditioning involves primarily response-consequence relationships in which a dog learns to volunteer a behavior in anticipation of pleasurable consequences (+R).

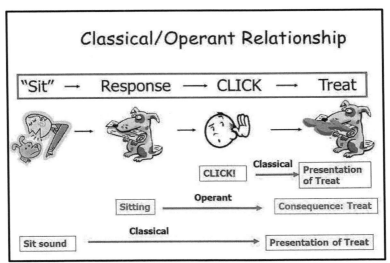

Both classical conditioning and operant conditioning take place during clicker training

- **CT is Classical:** Click (neutral stimulus) consistently precedes and predicts Treat (unconditioned stimulus). After several repetitions, the Click takes on the properties of the treat and is now said to be a conditioned stimulus. Trainers typically refer to it as "conditioned reinforcer" because the CT is used as a +R.

- **Sit/CT is Operant:** Dog offers a behavior (sit), which results in the presentation of CT (positive reinforcement). Dog says *"Yum! Sitting results in a treat! I like treats. I will increase the frequency that I offer a sit!"*

- **Cue/CT is Classical:** This last one is really cool, because it provides additional evidence for why our dogs SO enjoy clicker training. The voice cue *"Sit"* is added to the training process when the dog is reliably offering sit for CT. The trainer then begins to only CT when the dog offers the behavior in response to the voice cue (and no other time that the dog sits). Over time, as the dog attains proficiency (offers sit reliably in response to the cue), the cue *"Sit"* becomes a classically conditioned stimulus because it reliably precedes and predicts an opportunity for CT to the dog (with the operant sit behavior thrown in the middle). This means that the cues that the trainer uses with trained behaviors become imbued with the same characteristics as the click sound; *the voice cues themselves become something that the dog enjoys and looks forward to, because they are always paired with an opportunity to earn a CT.*

Take Away for Dog Folks: Happy Training!

REFERENCE: Clicker training diagram adapted from *Canine and Feline Behavior and Training: A Complete Guide to Understanding Our Two Best Friends*, LP Case, page 105, Cengage, 2010.

20
The Benjamin Franklin Effect

How doing something nice for someone else (or for one's dog) influences how we think about that individual.

Benjamin Franklin was a pretty amazing guy. The quintessential Renaissance Man, he was a scientist, inventor, author, musician, scholar, business man and politician. There are many popular stories and quotes from Franklin's life, but one in particular demonstrates his astute understanding of human behavior. In fact, this story became so well-known that it eventually led to what is now a well-known psychological phenomenon, aptly called, *The Benjamin Franklin Effect*.

The Story: Franklin first entered politics when he ran for and won election to the position of clerk of the state's general assembly. During his first term, like all politicians, Franklin made both a lot of friends as well as a few enemies. At the end of his term, one of those adversaries threatened Franklin's political career when he stood before the state legislature and delivered a long and scathing speech in opposition to Franklin's reelection. Although Franklin still won the election, he realized that the gentleman in question, as someone of substantial influence, would be better to have as a friend than as an enemy.

So, Franklin set about to change his adversary's opinion. He sent a letter to the man asking for a favor - the loan of a rare and highly sought after book that the man was known to have in his personal library. Flattered, Franklin's detractor immediately sent the book, along with a polite note, in response. Franklin read the book and returned it a week later with a note of thanks. According to Franklin's autobiography, the next time the legislature met, the man immediately approached and spoke cordially to Franklin. They discussed the book and several other common

119

interests. Franklin related that his former enemy and he eventually became close friends, a friendship that continued until the man's death. To quote from Franklin's autobiography *"He that has once done you a kindness will be more ready to do you another than he whom you yourself have obliged."*

The Benjamin Franklin Effect - Doing something nice for someone makes you like them more: Typically, we think that we do nice things for the people we like and we do less nice things to the people that we dislike. Similarly, we think that doing something nice for someone (i.e. loaning them a book), makes them like us better, not the opposite. However, it appears that, at least some of the time, the opposite is actually true. We come to think favorably about the people who we do nice things for, and equally, we come to dislike those who we treat poorly.

How the BF Effect works: Current self-perception theory tells us that our brains behave like an outside observer, continually watching what we do and then contriving explanations for those actions, which subsequently influence our beliefs about ourselves. I know. Weird. Sounds backwards, doesn't it? But, according to current research, this is the actual sequence for many of the things that we believe to be true about ourselves. Our observing brain doesn't like it when our actions don't match the beliefs we have about ourselves, a situation commonly referred to as *cognitive dissonance*. So, whenever your behavior is in conflict with your beliefs (for example if you do a favor for someone you may not like very much or vice versa, when you do something bad to someone you are supposed to care about), this conflict immediately sets off alarm bells in your brain. The brain has a clever response - it goes about changing how you *feel* in order to reduce the conflict and turn off the alarms.

So, if you believe that you don't like someone, but then you help them or do something nice for them, your brain simply changes how you think about that person. You start to think *"Gee, this guy is pretty cool; I actually do like him after all"*. Similarly, if you have been snarky toward someone you care about, your brain convinces you that the person must have deserved the poor treatment and......here is the really yucky part......*you start to find fault with the person and like him less.* A horrific and extreme example of this form of cognitive dissonance and its resolution is the way in which initially unwilling Nazi soldiers came to dehumanize and hate their Jewish victims.

The Research: There are many studies of cognitive dissonance and several specifically that have examined the Benjamin Franklin Effect. One of the first experiments invited volunteers to participate in a psychology experiment in which they would have the chance to win money (1). An actor pretending to be a scientist attempted to make the subjects dislike him by being rude and demanding as he administered a rigged series of tests to them. The subjects were successful in the tests regardless of how they answered and so all were awarded the promised money.

At the end of the session, the fake scientist stopped one-third of all the subjects as they were leaving and asked them to return the money. He told them he was paying for the experiment out of his own pocket and the study was in danger of losing its funding. All agreed to return the money (i.e. did the mean guy a favor). Another third left the room and a secretary (who they had not met before) asked if they would please donate their winnings back into the research department fund, providing the same reason. Again, everyone agreed. The final third simply left with their winnings. (Note: Remember The Steve Series: In this study design, the secretary group was a positive control and the group that kept their money was the negative control group).

The Results: The study objective, hidden from the participants, was to measure the volunteer's attitudes about the unpleasant scientist in the three different scenarios. All of the participants completed a questionnaire at the end of the day that asked them to rate the likeability of the scientist. True to the BF Effect, those participants who had done the scientist the favor directly rated him as significantly more likeable than either those who were asked by the secretary or those who left with their money. Even though they were treated very rudely, doing something nice for the obnoxious scientist caused people to think of him more positively.

At this point, you may be asking, "*What does any of this have to do with dogs*"?

Well, a lot, perhaps. Here's another study for you to ponder: In an experiment conducted at the University of North Carolina, participants were asked to teach a group of students to repeat a tapping pattern that they read from a set of instructions (2). They worked with each student individually and were instructed to use one of two teaching methods which were randomly assigned to each of their students. In one method, the teacher offered encouragement and praise when the learner repeated the tapping pattern correctly. In the second method, the teacher criticized and insulted the learner whenever they made mistakes. (Hmmm.....sound familiar trainers?). Afterward, the study participants who acted as teachers completed a questionnaire that included questions about how likable they found each of their students to be. Here are the results:

- The study participants rated the students who they had praised and encouraged as highly attractive, friendly, pleasant and likable.

- By comparison, they rated the students who they had insulted and berated as particularly unlikable and unattractive.

- The researchers concluded that the volunteer teachers' treatment of each student created their perception of that student. They liked the students who they were required to be kind to and they disliked the students who they were required to punish. This shows us that the Benjamin Franklin Effect works in both directions - kind behaviors create positive perceptions while hurtful behaviors lead to unfavorable perceptions.

Take Away for Dog Folks: Reading about the BF effect lead me to think about dogs and training (well okay, it is true that pretty much everything leads me to think about dogs). In this particular case, the Ben Franklin effect caused me to think more about the human side of the relationship rather than about the dogs themselves. Trainers who promote methods that emphasize positive reinforcement typically focus on the effects that these methods have upon the *dogs*. There is a general consensus that dogs who are trained with primarily positive reinforcement (+R) tend to be less stressed, are more willing and motivated to learn, and enjoy learning to a greater degree than dogs trained using negative reinforcement-based methods (-R).

However, we don't always consider the effects that these two approaches may have upon the *trainer*. The Benjamin Franklin Effect suggests that how we treat our dogs during training influences how we think about them as individuals - specifically, how much we like (or dislike) them. When we do nice things for our dogs in the form of treats, praise, petting and play to reinforce desired behaviors, such treatment may result in our *liking them more*. And, if we use harsh words, collar jerks or hitting in an attempt to change our dog's behavior, then, well, if good ol' Ben is correct, *we will start to like our dog less*. If the Ben Franklin Effect is correct, we are heavily (and unconsciously) inclined to like the dogs who we treat well (use +R) and to dislike the dogs who we treat poorly (-R).

Think about it. When you see someone yelling at their dog.......does that person really appear to *like* that dog? Is cognitive dissonance (and the BF effect) leading them to conclude that their dog *must be bad, poorly behaved, dumb, unlikable, unattractive, since he is deserving of such correction?* Similarly, does the regular use of positive reinforcement, telling our dogs "Yippee, you did it!! You are SO smart and so very good!" subconsciously also encourage us to love our dogs more and to think more kind-ly about them?

Be nice. Be kind. Do favors. Ben says you will love your dog more for it.

CITED STUDIES:

1. Jecker J, Landy D. Liking a person as a function of doing him a favour. *Human Relations* 1969 22:371-378.

2. Shopler J, Compere J. Effects of being kind or harsh to anoth-er on liking. *Journal of Personality and Social Psychology* 1971; 20:155-159.

21
The Consequences of Consequences

The types of consequences that we use during training appear to have consequences of their own – on the relationships that we have with our dogs.

Operant learning is all about consequences. Most trainers and behaviorists are well-versed in the uses of pleasant and aversive stimuli as dog training consequences. These can be constructed into a 2 x 2 matrix that includes the type of stimulus (desirable/pleasant or aversive/unpleasant) as one factor and the intended behavioral change (increase or decrease response frequency) as the second factor (1).

TYPE OF STIMULUS	BEHAVIORAL CHANGE	
	INCREASE FREQUENCY	*DECREASE FREQUENCY*
DESIRABLE	*Positive Reinforcement (add stimulus)*	*Negative Punishment (remove stimulus)*
AVERSIVE	*Negative Reinforcement (remove stimulus)*	*Positive Punishment (add stimulus)*

In all animals, including dogs, learning occurs when one of these four consequences lead to a change in behavior:

- **Positive reinforcement (+R):** Delivery (acquisition) of a desirable stimulus (food treat, praise, petting, play) results in an increase in the response. Example: Dog *increases* "sit" response to acquire petting and a food treat.

125

- **Negative Reinforcement (-R):** Disappearance (avoidance) of an aversive stimulus (head collar pressure, collar jerk, harsh voice) results in an increase in the response that allows the dog to avoid the unpleasant stimulus. Example: Dog increases "sit" response to avoid pressure applied to head collar or collar jerk (or to avoid a horrible "ehhhh" sound emanating from the trainer. How do people produce that sound, anyway?)

- **Positive Punishment (+P):** Delivery of an aversive stimulus results in a decrease in response. Example: Dog decreases standing/lying down/moving away from a sit position to avoid pressure applied to head collar or collar jerk (or the horrible "ehhhh" sound).

- **Negative Punishment (-P):** Removal of a desirable stimulus results in a decrease in the response. Example: Dog decreases standing/lying down to avoid losing access to food treats, petting praise attained whilst sitting quietly.

The Hypothesis: There is a general (but certainly not universal) consensus among trainers and behaviorists that training methods that emphasize positive reinforcement (+R) are more effective and more humane than those that emphasize the use of aversive stimuli (i.e. "corrections"). To date, there is some evidence in the scientific literature that supports +R methods as more effective than negative reinforcement (-R) or punishment (see Essay 18, "*Yogi Bear Dogs*"). And now, there is a study that examines the effects of these two different training approaches upon dogs' levels of stress and their relationships with their owners (2).

The Study: Stephanie Deldalle and Florence Gaunet of the University of Paris-Nord and the Laboratoire de Psychologie Cognitive in France conducted an exploratory study that observed two dog training schools and their students during a series of advanced training classes. One school used primarily +R methods in the form of food treats, praise and petting to increase desired behaviors in the dogs. The second school used primarily -R methods in the form of collar corrections (pressure/jerks) and physical manipulation (pushing the dog into a sit). Neither the schools' instructors nor their students were aware of the study's objectives or that their school had been selected because of the type of methods that were used to train dogs.

A group of 24 owner-dog pairs training at the +R school (hereafter +RS) and a group of 26 owner-dog pairs at the -R school (hereafter -RS) were studied. The dogs represented a variety of breeds and ranged in age from 8 months to 7 years. One researcher attended two sessions of a one-hour advanced class at each school and collected data for 50 minutes during each visit. Data collected included the owner's behavior and the dog's response and body postures when walking on a loose lead and when responding to the "sit" command. Within each session the frequencies of +R and -R stimuli used by the observed owners were also recorded. Owners were asked to complete a questionnaire at the end of the session.

Results: No differences in owner demographics (sex, age, socioeconomic status, etc.) or dog characteristics were found between the +RS and the -RS groups. Training results were classified by activity:

- **Response to sit command:** Dogs who were trained using primarily -R showed significantly more mouth licking (38 % vs. 8 % of dogs), yawning (12 % vs. 0 % of dogs), and lowered body postures (46 % vs. 8 %) when compared with dogs trained with +R. All of these behaviors are associated with stress and anxiety in dogs. Collectively, 65 percent of dogs in the -RS group demonstrated at least one stress-related behavior, compared with only 8 percent of dogs in the +RS group. And that is not all. Significantly more dogs in the +RS group offered spontaneous gaze to their owners during the sit command when compared with dogs from the -RS group

(88 % vs. 33 %), a behavior that is interpreted as an invitation to visually interact and a positive relationship.

- **Walking on a loose lead:** Although not statistically significant, more dogs in the -RS demonstrated lowered body postures while walking when compared with dogs enrolled in the +RS (15 % vs. 4 %). However, reduced body posture while walking was relatively uncommon in both schools. Similar to their response during the sit command, significantly more dogs in the +RS group offered spontaneous gaze to their owner during heeling compared with dogs in the -RS group (63 % vs. 4 %).

Take Away for Dog Folks: It is important to note this was a preliminary and exploratory study that compared students who were training their dogs at one of two possible schools. This methodology can allow comparison of the behavior of dogs trained using two sets of training instructions (which is exactly what the researchers did), but *cannot* be used to make general conclusions about training *schools* that use different methods because only one school of each type was studied. Although this may seem to be a minor point, it is an important one that cautions us to take care when interpreting the results of this study. (For a refresher on the need to study groups rather than single entities, see The Steve Series essays in Part 1). Keeping this in mind, the results of this study suggest (but do not prove) that:

- An emphasis upon negative reinforcement when training dogs to perform basic manners exercises (sit, walk on lead) can cause stress and anxiety in dogs, demonstrated as reduced body posture, tongue flicks, yawning, and avoiding eye contact.

- Conversely, an emphasis upon positive reinforcement may improve a dog's confidence and relationship with her owner, as evidenced by offering voluntary eye contact (and by the absence of the aforementioned stress-related behaviors).

- Perhaps most importantly (and unique to this study design): All of the dogs in this study had been in training for at least several months and were enrolled in an advanced class. Those dogs who were trained using -R were most likely to respond with stress to the owner's verbal command "sit". *The researchers suggested that the training itself and its attendant commands/cues had become a conditioned aversive stimulus for these dogs. In other words, there were significant consequences to the type of consequences that were used during training.*

CITED STUDY:

Deldalle S, Gaunet F. Effects of two training methods on stress-related behaviors of the dog (*Canis familiaris*) and on the dog-owner relationship. *Journal of Veterinary Behavior: Clinical Applications and Research* 2014; 9:58-65.

22
The Quiz

How would you prefer to learn math?
More about consequences.

Imagine that you have enrolled in a college math course. You have been attending lectures for several weeks and although the material is quite difficult, you feel that the instructor has been explaining the concepts very clearly and that you have been able to learn a great deal from his lectures. You have completed and handed in three homework assignments and received over 90 % on each one. You are feeling pretty confident about your math skills and are happy with what you have learned so far in the course.

This afternoon, you enter the lecture hall for the weekly lecture and the instructor informs the class of 50 students that he will be administering a surprise quiz. He has two options for taking the quiz; one in Classroom A and the other in Classroom B. The instructor has randomly assigned students to each room. He tells you that the questions on the quiz are exactly the same in each room, but the consequences for answering quiz questions are slightly different.

Classroom A: There is an enormous bowl of candy sitting on the front desk. The quiz instructions are as follows: The instructor will put an equation to be solved up on the overhead screen. When a student has correctly solved the problem, he or she should raise a hand and provide the answer aloud. If the student answers correctly, he or she will receive a candy. The student may then either remain to try for another correct answer (and another candy!) or can be dismissed with the remainder of the day off. If the student provides an incorrect answer, he or she is simply asked to try again. All students must answer one question correctly to complete the quiz.

Classroom B: The chairs in this room have been electronically wired so that a mild but quite unpleasant electric shock can be sent to each chair by the instructor. The quiz instructions are as follows: The instructor will put an equation to be solved up on the overhead screen. When a student has correctly solved the problem, he or she should raise a hand and provide the answer aloud. If the student answers correctly, he or she is dismissed and may have the remainder of the day off. If the student provides an incorrect answer, he or she will receive an electric shock and must remain in the class and try again. All students must answer one question correctly to complete the quiz.

Which room would you rather be in? And......Which room's approach would further encourage your interest in learning math?

Dogs may not learn math, but they do respond to aversive and pleasurable stimuli in the same manner as do math students.

REFERENCE: Parable adapted from *Canine and Feline Behavior and Training: A Complete Guide to Under-standing Our Two Best Friends*, LP Case, page 107-108, Cengage, 2010.

23
Is it Time for the Extinction of Extinction?

A new look at a popular approach to eliminating un-wanted behaviors (such as jumping up to greet) in dogs.

Jumping up on people is a frequently cited complaint that dog owners make to dog trainers. Although it can be a frustrating problem for owners, it is important to note that the underlying cause of jumping up is, in most cases, is simply a dog who is exuberantly saying "*Hello! How are ya! How about some lovin?*" And of course, a contributing cause is that we humans are frequently inconsistent in our responses; some of the time we enjoy it and encourage it, and in other circumstances (such as when Muffin knocks over Grandma or places muddy feet on a visitor's white dress) we are not quite so happy about the paws that are suddenly planted on our chest.

Although other trainers' opinions certainly vary, my general view of jumping up is that "*Yes, dogs do this. Yes, many owners dislike it and would like to stop it and we can help them with that. However, in the overall scheme of things, having a dog who is a bit too friendly and exuberant really isn't such a terrible problem to have now, is it*"? So, my own training school's approach to the problem is to first frame it in terms of what it actually is.......a dog being friendly. Maybe even an overly excited, young, goofy maniac of a dog, but still, he is just trying to say hello, albeit with an enthusiastic demeanor.

Once that is settled, we address ways to modify the dog's behavior to reduce jumping up to greet. One approach that trainers and behaviorists use to reduce or eliminate unwanted behaviors is to train the dog to offer an alternate response that is incompatible with the undesired behavior, a technique called "response substitution". For example, in the case of jumping up to greet, we teach Mr. Exuberance to "sit for his lovin'" rather than to jump up for it. First the owner, then eventually visitors, crouch to greet and reinforce the dog with treats and affection, eventually shaping the behavior to achieve sitting for greeting. Over time, the person will remain in an upright position whilst continuing to reinforce sit or simply "keep four feet on the floor".

An alternative approach is extinction. Extinction refers to purposefully and consistently preventing reinforcement of the unwanted behavior until the dog stops offering the unwanted behavior (i.e. the unwanted behavior is extinguished). Using the example of jumping up, this means removing *the person*. Greeting the dog (providing petting, love, interaction) is what positively reinforces and thus maintains jumping up. So, extinction involves telling the owner to ignore the dog by turning her back, backing away, or walking away from the dog whenever he attempts to greet by jumping up. (Note: In this particular example, extinction is almost indistinguishable from negative punishment).

Does Extinction Work? Actually putting this technique into practice presents some problems, however. It is associated with what traditional behaviorists (of the Skinner "can't talk about internal emotional states" ilk) refer to as an "extinction burst", and what trainers typically call "frustration and emotional distress". In practice this means that the dog increases his bid for attention by following the owner and jumping more emphatically, becoming more active and frantic, barking and whining, nipping or mouthing. Generally, you end up with a mess - a dog who went from jumping and happy to jumping and distressed and who may have added one or two new and equally undesirable behaviors to his repertoire.

Why We Need Data: This discussion begs (pun intended) the question - Does extinction work well as a practical training approach with dogs? More importantly, even if it does effectively reduce unwanted behaviors, does it come at the cost of unneces-

133

sary emotional stress and the risk of creating new problems? Regardless of my personal opinion of using extinction in dog training, all that I really could say about its use until now has come from personal experience with my clients and their dogs and discussions with other trainers. (And, in case you have not caught it, my personal opinion is that it does not work well and causes unneeded distress and anxiety in the dog). Moreover, despite the existence of an effective alternate technique (response substitution), ignoring a dog who jumps up continues to be frequently recommended to pet owners by a wide variety of trainers, behaviorists, bloggers, veterinarians and authors.

The Study: Until recently, there were no data that specifically examined the use of extinction with pet dogs. However, building on work from previously published research, a group of investigators in Argentina recently asked the question "*Does the use of extinction with dogs produce an aversive emotional state [even while it may effectively reduce the targeted behavior]*?" (1,2). In other words, does the use of extinction in dog training cause emotional distress?

Altogether, 45 dogs living as companions in homes with people were studied. The study protocol included three phases: The first was a warm-up during which the dog met the trainer and became accustomed to the training area. The second was the training (acquisition) phase. The trainer used dried liver treats to positively reinforce "gazing behavior" (looking into the trainer's face) each time that the dog offered it. Three sessions lasting 2 minutes each were completed with each dog. The liver treats were kept in a container, located on a shelf, next to the trainer. The third stage was the extinction phase. The experimenter continued to stand near the shelf but now ignored the dog when he/she offered the previously reinforced gazing behavior. Three extinction sessions were conducted for each dog. Each session was video recorded and rated by an impartial observer following the sessions.

Results: Using extinction significantly reduced the targeted behavior (gazing), but also led to an increase in behaviors that are associated with frustration. These included withdrawing from the trainer, lying down, increased movement (ambulation), whining, sniffing (often considered to be a displacement behavior), and avoiding the trainer. The researchers note that these results are especially relevant given the common use of extinction for discouraging unwanted behaviors in pet dogs.

Take Away for Dog Folks: For trainers, this study (and the researcher's previous work) showed that extinction can effectively reduce a previously reinforced behavior in pet dogs. The results also showed that, while effective, extinction causes stress and potentially leads to displacement behaviors that can be problematic. I finished reading this article thinking about two important differences between the study protocol and the use of extinction in everyday life with the dogs who live with us:. These are:

1. The trainer in this study, while friendly and pleasant to the dogs, was unfamiliar and had no previous relationship or enduring bond with the dogs.

2. The targeted behavior, "gazing" was trained for a very short period (6 minutes!), and so had a very short and weak reinforcement history with the subject dogs.

Together, these two facts suggest that the behavior that was trained (gazing) and subsequently extinguished was not a persistent behavior that held a lot of significance to the dog. It had an almost ridiculously short reinforcement history and involved a person who really held no importance to the dog. Yet, extinction still caused frustration and emotional distress in the dogs in this study. Wow.

Up on my Soapbox

Soapbox Time: So, one can imagine the degree of frustration felt by a dog who loves his people (and visitors) and who has a long history of being reinforced for showing what he considers to be just normal doggy affection (jumping up), when suddenly, all of the positive stuff abruptly stops. His pals begin to ignore him completely, turning their backs, walking away, not speaking to him, whenever he attempts to say hello.

Personally, I found the results of this small study compelling if simply to suggest that it may be time to consider the extinction of extinction in dog training. This is certainly not a difficult call, given that we have available other, more effective and less stress-inducing approaches, such as response substitution. Although training a dog to sit for greeting takes a bit more time, patience, and tolerance (jumping up is NOT the end of the world, after all), certainly it is preferable to using a technique that causes emotional distress to the dog, has the potential to cause other problems, and removes yet another opportunity to interact positively with our dogs.

CITED STUDIES:

1. Bentosela M, Barrera GT, Jakovcevic A, et al. Effects of reinforcement, reinforce omission and extinction on a communicative response in domestic dogs (*Canis familiaris*). *Behavioral Processes* 2008; 78:464-469.

2. Jakovcevic A, Elgier AM, Mustaca AE, Bentosela M. Frustration behaviors in domestic dogs. *Journal of Applied Animal Welfare Science* 2013; 16:19-34.

24
Hey Teacher! Leave those Dogs Alone!

Is taking a student's dog from them to demonstrate training techniques a helpful exercise? A new study asks the dogs how they feel about it.

It is a fairly common practice among dog trainers who teach group classes to "borrow" one of their student's dogs to demonstrate a training technique or learning concept. Opinions of this practice vary. Proponents say that it helps owners to observe their own dog being handled by an instructor or responding to someone else, while opponents argue that it can appear as instructor grandstanding, may embarrass the owner, and can confuse or even frighten the dog. First, make note that this is not an issue that I feel so strongly about that I would march on Washington about it or wear a sandwich board in protest on a busy street corner. However, I do place myself firmly in the *"don't take my students' dogs to demo"* camp. My reasons are not as much to do with embarrassing the owner (which admittedly can happen), as they are concerned with the dog's welfare and comfort level and with being consistent regarding my own personal beliefs about our relationships with dogs.

Here is What I Mean: When out and about with my own dogs, I neither enjoy nor tolerate a stranger approaching us to say hello to my dogs, and then instead of greeting them politely and spending some time getting to know them through petting and chit-chat with me, the person instead barks out some command. Although these commands are usually benign (sit or "shake" seem to be popular), they grate on me and annoy my dogs. And of course, if my dogs do not instantly snap-to and comply, the person barks again, more loudly. Fun times.

Not only is such human behavior unpleasant to be around, I see no reason at all that my dogs should be arbitrarily required to listen to someone who they do not know and have absolutely no relationship with. Therefore, since I personally do not want other people deciding that my dogs are required to listen to them, why would I foist such a practice upon my own training school students and their dogs? Instead, the policy at my training school is for instructors to use our own dogs for demonstration purposes or if our dogs are not present for the class, we enlist the aid of the invisible dog, "Muffin" (who always listens).

What do the Dogs Think? I have not yet found any research that examines how dog owners feel about having someone else train, work with or command their dog. However, a study was recently published that asked how *dogs* feel about this (1).

The Study: The researchers were interested in finding out if the presence or absence of a dog's owner and the familiarity of a tester influences a dog's behavior and performance during various types of cognitive testing. They were particularly interested in teasing out context-specific effects. In other words, do dogs react differently to familiar versus unfamiliar handlers depending on what you are asking of them or the situation in which they find themselves? Here is how they studied this:

- **Dogs and handlers:** A group of 20 adult, well socialized dogs and their owners participated in the study. In addition, each owner selected a friend or relative who their dog knew well (familiar person). The unfamiliar person was one of the female researchers, who had not previously met any of the dogs. (Because gender has been shown to have a significant effect upon behavior, this factor was controlled in this study by enrolling only female owners and friends).

- **Tests:** A set of eight behavior tests was administered to each dog. Some of the tests measured the dog's response to separation from the owner or other stressors, and others exam-

139

ined the dog's response to obedience commands or handling. In addition, two locations were used; an unfamiliar, indoor testing area and a familiar outdoor area. Each dog was tested by their owner, the familiar person, and the unfamiliar person.

Results: Both the human handler's familiarity and the context (type of test and setting) significantly influenced dogs' behavior and response to commands. While the dogs consistently discriminated between their owner and the unfamiliar person and always preferred the owner, discrimination between the owner and the familiar person was affected by context. Here are the highlights:

- **Choice and confidence:** Unsurprisingly, when allowed to choose between their owner and the other two handlers, dogs consistently showed clear preference for their owner. They also showed a greater tendency to interact with others when the owner was present, a phenomenon that has been observed in other studies and is referred to as the "*secure base*" effect. It appears that owners provide their dog with a feeling of security and enhanced confidence, which in turn encourages the dog to explore new situations and people. In the absence of the owner, dogs' behaviors tended to be more inhibited.

- **Stressful situations:** Dogs distinguished strongly between their owner and the other two testers (familiar and unfamiliar) in situations that were stressful, such as separation or the approach of a threatening human. Most compelling? The presence of the friend could not sufficiently substitute for the presence of the owner in any of these settings.

- **Play:** Although most of the dogs would play with all three testers, they spent more time playing with their owner and orienting to the toy (ball) that the owner was holding than they did with either the familiar or unfamiliar tester. During play, the dogs did not show a preference for the familiar over the unfamiliar person, but reacted similarly to both.

- **Response to commands:** Overall, dogs responded most consistently to the owner rather than the other testers for basic commands of come, sit and down. However, the average time that it took for dogs to respond to commands (called latency) was not different between owners and the familiar person. In contrast, dogs took significantly longer to respond to commands if they were given by the unfamiliar person.

Take Away for Dog Folks: Given these results, let's return to the question of whether or not it is helpful for an instructor to take a student's dog from them to demonstrate a technique or to help them to train their dog. Certainly in many cases, an instructor becomes well-known to the dogs in his or her class and is recognized by most of the dogs as a friend. (This is especially true if the instructor regularly carries yummy treats in her training pouch and is very generous with those treats). Still, even knowing this, the results of this study suggest that dogs perform best when they have their owner close at hand to act as their secure base. When a bit stressed (as group classes can often be), it really does not matter if the person who takes the dog is familiar or not (or is a better trainer than the owner). Dogs still prefer to be with and respond best to their owner. So, if you are in the habit of taking others' dogs from them to demonstrate or train, keep in mind that even if you are more skilled, even if you can train the behavior faster, and even if the dog performs well for you, this may not be the dog's preference. And if we are in the business of building strong bonds between dogs and their people, this may be something to consider.

CITED STUDY:

Kerepesi A, Doka A, Miklosi A. Dogs and their human companions: The effect of familiarity on dog-human interactions. *Behavioural Processes* 2014; In Press.

Part 4 –
Dogs & Their People

25
I Yawn for Your Love

Is yawning in dogs a form of social contagion, a sign of stress, or both?

Vinny, my Brittany, yawns a lot. He yawns first thing in the morning when he rises, in the evening when he is tired, and many times in between. We notice this because Vinny emits an adorable little squeaky sound whenever he launches a particularly wide and emotive yawn. We also know that Vinny seems to be highly susceptible to contagious yawning. If Mike or I or one of the other dogs yawn when we are close by, Vinny immediately joins in.

So, consider my delight when I found a series of research studies that examined the phenomenon of yawning in dogs and their people. The primary objectives of these studies were to determine if dog yawning, traditionally believed to reflect the presence of moderate stress in dogs, is in actuality (or additionally) a reflection of social contagion and empathy.

Background Information: In humans, contagious yawning is a well-established phenomenon. Not only are most of us easily induced to open wide when someone nearby emits a yawn, there is evidence that even just hearing a yawn noise or watching others yawning on a video are sufficient to trigger a yawn response. (Indeed, I would venture that simply reading the previous two sentences, in which the word "yawn" occurs six times, caused more than a few readers to......yawn).

There are several theories that attempt to explain why yawning is socially contagious. At the simplest cognitive level, group yawning may just reflect unconscious mimicry, a form of priming. This is the most parsimonious view as it does not require

143

emotional attachment between the yawner and the "yawnee" and does not require the ability to empathize (or have a "theory of mind"). Alternate theories place contagious yawning somewhat higher on the social cognition scale and suggest that it represents an involuntary empathic response. In other words, people yawn when others do because they feel the same (i.e. empathize). According to this view, people should be more likely to yawn in response to others who they know well and have an emotional bond with than when they are with unfamiliar yawners. In recent years, data show that this is indeed true. Additional studies show that people who score highly on psychological tests of empathy are more susceptible to contagious yawning than are those who score low on tests of empathy. This evidence has tipped the evidence scale towards the empathy theory (at least for people).

What about Dogs? Although spontaneous yawning occurs in many mammals, contagious yawning has only been described in humans, chimpanzees, and in recent years - in dogs. Studies with dogs have asked three primary questions:

- Do dogs exhibit *cross-species* contagious yawning? In other words, does seeing a human yawn increase the likelihood that a dog will respond with a yawn?

- If it does occur, is it a type of empathic response? Are dogs more likely to yawn in response to someone they know and share an emotional bond with than they are in response to a stranger? If so, does contagious yawning have a communication function?

- And, a related question that is of interest to most trainers - may contagious (or spontaneous) yawning be simply a stress response in dogs that occurs during times of low or moderate anxiety? And, if so, is there a contagious component to it?

144

The Studies: The first published study of dog yawns appeared in 2008 in a paper entitled "*Dogs Catch Human Yawns*" (1). The researchers examined a group of 29 dogs and found that 21 of the dogs (72 %) demonstrated contagious yawning when sitting near an unfamiliar (yawning) person. The control group (eye contact plus non-yawning mouth movements) elicited zero yawns. This was pretty impressive, seeing that rates reported in humans range between 45 and 60 % and chimps come in at a paltry 33%. Although this study demonstrated yawn contagion, the design of the study did not allow the researchers to determine if the dogs were yawning as an expression of empathy or as a stress/anxiety response. Other researchers decided to study this further:

- **Nope, ain't happenin':** A 2011 study compared yawn rates in dogs who were exposed to the yawns of either their owner, a stranger, or another dog (2). They also compared pet dogs living in homes with rescue dogs living in a shelter. Although they saw a bit of yawning (~ 26 % of dogs), the rates did not differ significantly from control rates for any of these conditions. These researchers concluded that they found no evidence for empathy-based contagious yawning in dogs.

- **Listen......there it is!** Another study took a different approach. They recorded the sound of yawning in 29 dog owners and then played these recordings back to each owner's respective dog (3). The dogs were also exposed to the yawn sounds of an unfamiliar person and to familiar/unfamiliar non-yawn sounds (controls). Hearing the sound of yawning caused a response in 41 percent of the dogs and the sound of a familiar yawn elicited significantly more yawns than did the sound of an unfamiliar yawn. (Additional analysis of the data collected in this study suggested that stress-induced yawning was not an underlying cause of dog yawning, lending support for the social (empathy-based) theory [4]).

- **I yawn for you:** This 2013 study was specifically designed to test whether contagious yawning in dogs was a result of stress or if it reflected an empathic response (5). The researchers monitored dogs' heart rates during each condition as a measure of physiological stress. Testing 25 dogs, they found that dogs did indeed demonstrate contagious yawning, that dogs yawned significantly more frequently in response to their owner than in response to an unfamiliar person, and that heart rates did not increase significantly during the experiment. Their results lend support to the hypothesis that dogs show contagious yawning with humans and that this behavior is socially modulated (i.e. empathy-based) rather than stress-based.

- **But wait......do dogs also stress yawn contagiously?** The most recent study, published in 2014, shows just how complicated the dog yawning story may actually be (6). Changing things up a bit, this group of researchers worked with a group of 60 shelter dogs and exposed them to a yawning (unfamiliar) experimenter. They measured both yawn responses and salivary cortisol levels, which like heart rate, are expected to rise during periods of physiological stress. Contagious yawning in the shelter dogs occurred in only 12 (20 %) of the dogs, but interestingly, it was those dogs (the yawners) whose cortisol levels were increased. These results suggest that stress yawns can also occur contagiously.

Take Away for Dog Folks: Taken together, the results of these studies suggest that yawning in dogs may be context-specific, having different functions depending upon setting and situation. Similar to several other species, dogs do appear to yawn during periods of mild stress, possibly as a displacement behavior. In these cases, the yawn is accompanied by other communicative signs of tension such as a lowered body posture, panting, pacing or whining. [Note: While some posit that dogs yawn as a signal to "calm" other dogs or people, there is no empirical evidence to support this belief]. The data in these studies suggest that a stress yawn may also occur "contagiously" when faced with an unknown person in a new setting, perhaps as a result of the person (or her yawns) causing an increase in tension in the dog. Conversely, contagious yawning that occurs in a relaxed and happy dog, typically in response to a familiar person, may signify a type of social communication that reveals some level of empathic response. In those cases, what exactly is being communicated ("*I'm tired too*" or "*This TV show is boring; can we please turn Lassie on*", or "*Let's go for ice cream!*") is still open to debate.

CITED STUDIES:

1. Joly-Mascheroni RM, Senju A, Shephred AJ. Dogs catch human yawns. *Biology Letters* 2008; 4:446-448.

2. O'Hara SJ, Reeve AV. A test of the yawning contagion and emotional connectedness hypothesis in dogs, *Canis familiaris. Animal Behaviour* 2011; 81:335-340.

3. Silva K, Bessa J, Sousa L. Auditory contagious yawning in domestic dogs (*Canis familiaris*): first evidence for social modulation. *Animal Cognition* 2012; 15:721-724.

4. Silva K, Bessa J, deSousa L. Familiarity-connected or stress-based contagious yawning in domestic dogs (*Canis familiaris*)? Some additional data. *Animal Cognition* 2013; 16:1007-1009.

5. Romero T, Konno A, Hasegawa T. Familiarity bias and physiological responses in contagious yawning by dogs support link to empathy. *PLoS ONE* 2013: 8(8):e71365.

6. Buttner AP, Strasser R. Contagious yawning, social cognition, and arousal: An investigation of the processes underlying shelter dogs' responses to human yawns. *Animal Cognition* 2014; 17:95-104.

26
Fear Itself

How skilled are dog owners and non-owners at detecting signs of fear and stress in dogs?

Recently, on the drive home from our annual vacation in Bar Harbor, Maine, Vinny suddenly and inexplicably awoke from a sound sleep and began to tremble, pant, pace, and obsessively lick at the sides of his travel crate. When I crawled back over the seat to find out what was wrong, his eyes were "squinty" and he avoided looking at me as he continued to lick and pant. My husband, Mike, immediately pulled over to a rest area and we got Vinny out of the car. As soon as he was on the ground and moving about, Vinny relaxed, looked at us calmly, gave each of us a nice Brittany hug, and off we went for a little walk.

Perplexed, we thought that maybe he had to eliminate (nope, no urgency there), was feeling carsick (no signs), or had had a bad dream (who knows?). Within less than a minute, our sweet Brittany was his typical happy self, showing no signs at all of distress. We loaded all of the dogs back into the car and Vinny continued the journey home with no further incident. We still are not sure what triggered this odd stress episode in our boy. Several weeks later, he has not had a recurrence and is healthy and happy, but we continue to monitor him carefully both at home and when he is traveling with us.

Recognizing Stress and Fear: It is important for dog owners to recognize and respond to signs of stress and fear in our dogs. If we are sensitive to their emotional states and are accurate in our interpretations, we can respond appropriately to situations in which a dog is uncomfortable, stressed, or frightened. Because nonspecific signs of stress can be the first signs of illness or injury, attending to these promptly may help us to get our dogs the medical attention that they need before conditions worsen or escalate into an emergency. It is well known that perceiving and understanding the emotions of others is a basic human social skill. We use these perceptions on a daily basis when we interact with other people - family members, friends, and even strangers. Interestingly, while most of us are capable on some level of reading the emotional states of other humans, studies have shown that these abilities vary tremendously among individuals. Similarly, because many of us share our lives with dogs, it follows that we use these same skills when interpreting the emotions of our canine friends. Let's look at two studies that examined the cues that we use and our levels of accuracy when we perceive fear and stress in our canine companions.

Study 1: The first was conducted by researchers in the Department of Psychology at Columbia University in New York (1). The study team produced a series of video clips of dogs and embedded them in an on-line survey. Participants viewed the videos and then were asked to classify each dog's emotional state using one of five possible descriptors (angry, fearful, happy, sad, or neutral). The first four of these are called "primary emotions" and were selected because research has supported the existence of these emotions in dogs and other animals. Although the study participants had 5 choices, the videos in the study only showed dogs demonstrating two possible emotions, either happiness or fear. All of the videos had been pre-categorized into the two emotion categories by a panel of dog behavior experts prior to the start of the study.

After identifying each dog's emotion, participants were asked to describe the specific features of the dog that they felt led them to their conclusion. For example, if a person classified a dog as showing happiness, she might say that the dog's facial expression, ear set, and wagging tail were important features that conveyed this state to her. Last, the participants were asked to rate the level of difficulty that they experienced while attempting to interpret the emotions of each dog and to provide an estimate of overall confidence in their accuracy.

Results: Over 2000 people completed the survey and were divided into four dog experience categories based upon their dog ownership and professional histories. These were non-owners, owners, dog professionals with less than 10 years of experience, and professionals with more than 10 years of experience. It was somewhat surprising to find that the vast majority of people who completed the survey, more than 90 percent, correctly identified happy dogs in the video clips, regardless of the person's level of dog experience. This means that most people, even those who have never owned a dog, could look at a happy dog and see.....*a happy dog!* This is good news.

However, when it came to recognizing fear in dogs, the news was not quite so positive. While more than 70 percent of dog professionals correctly identified the fearful dogs, this proportion dropped to 60 percent of dog owners, and to only *35 percent* of non-owners. Put another way, this means that 40 percent of dog owners and 65 percent of non-owners were unable to correctly identify signs of fear and stress in an unfamiliar dog. Moreover, a substantial number of the non-owners (17 percent, or about one in six people) misclassified a fearful dog as a happy dog. This statistic is especially troubling, given the potential dangerous outcome of such mistakes. A person who approaches a dog who they believe to be friendly but who actually is fearful, will at the very least increase the dog's fear and distress and could potentially cause a defensive response in the dog, leading to a snap or bite.

The features that participants used to make their decisions also varied with experience level. A person's tendency to focus on a dog's facial features (eyes, mouth, ears) increased significantly along with experience. Inexperienced participants used primarily the dog's tail and body posture to inform them about the dog's emotional state. Conversely, more experienced people identified both body postures and facial expressions as important features when assessing a dog.

Benefits of Experience: Interestingly, but perhaps not surprisingly, the results of this study are consistent with studies of human abilities to perceive and interpret the expression of emotions in other people. We are generally more sensitive to and more accurate at interpreting happy facial expressions in other people than we are when responding to fearful expressions. Moreover, while social experience seems to have little effect upon our responses to happy faces (we show a proficiency to do this at a very young age), having varied and extensive social experience is an important factor in determining our success at perceiving fear and stress in other people. In dogs, this study tells us that dog-related training and experience enhance our tendency to pay attention to dogs' facial expressions along with their body postures and enhances our ability to correctly perceive fear.

Study 2: While the first study provided a general test of how people perceive fear in unfamiliar dogs, the second examined the ability of dog owners to recognize signs of stress in their *own* dogs (2). This study was conducted by researchers at the University of Pisa in Italy with a group of almost 1200 dog owners recruited through veterinary clinics. Participants first completed a questionnaire in which they were asked general questions about stress in dogs and its potential health and behavioral consequences. They then identified what they believed to be signs of stress in dogs and estimated the level of stress in their own dog. More than half of the owners (60 %) were found to have a clear understanding of what stress is and how it can affect a dog's emotional state and health. However, about 20 percent of owners (one in five) believed that experiencing stress had no negative physical or emotional consequences on dogs. (In other words, while they agreed that it occurred, they thought it was no big deal).

The behaviors that owners most frequently identified as reflecting stress in their dog included trembling, whining/crying, excessive barking, and panting. In contrast, very few owners identified more subtle behaviors such as avoiding eye contact, turning away, yawning, or nose licking as signs of stress in dogs. Those owners who self-reported as being highly concerned with their dog's stress level were more likely to identify these less obvious signs as important. Overall though, owners tended to miss many of the facial expressions (squinty eyes, avoiding eye contact, changes to ear set, retracted commissures) that most trainers immediately look for when they are assessing a dog's stress level. Like the first study, this suggests that it is these more subtle facial cues of stress and fear that may be missed if a person is only paying attention to the more obvious body posture signs.

Take Away for Dog Folks: These two studies provide complementary information about the behavior cues that people pay attention to when attempting to decipher a dog's emotional state. The first showed that even inexperienced people were able to correctly identify a dog who was feeling happy. However, perceptions of fear were strongly correlated to how much prior experience a person has had with dogs. As experience level increased, not only were people more likely to be correct, but they also were more likely to pay attention to a dog's facial expressions than were people who did not spend much time with dogs. We also learned that dog owners are more likely to focus attention on their dog's body posture, vocalizations and movements than on the more subtle signs of stress that involve a dog's facial expressions and eyes.

Accurately recognizing fear and stress in dogs is an important skill set to have. Understanding our own dog's emotional state allows us to respond by helping him out of situations that cause fear and reducing or eliminating triggers of stress when they are under our control. For trainers and behaviorists, working with owners who are sensitive to their dog's stress response promotes the development of a more effective training and management plan. On a societal level we all benefit from a universal understanding of the behaviors, body postures and facial expressions that convey happiness versus fear or stress in dogs. Correct interpretation of a dog's behavior is always enhanced by attending to both body posture and facial expressions. However, interpretation of dogs' facial expressions may not come naturally to many people. This knowledge emphasizes the importance of teaching the subtleties of canine facial expressions in training classes, behavior education courses, and bite prevention programs. Moreover, the statistic suggesting that one in five owners do not consider the effects of stress in their dogs to be of negative consequence tells us that education is also needed regarding the health and welfare impacts of stress and fear on our dogs' well-being and quality of life.

Here at home, Mike and I are still uncertain about what caused Vinny's acute stress response during our vacation trip. As Vinny has aged he has become somewhat more sound sensitive, which is not unusual. However, even though we responded quickly at the time and he apparently recovered, we did not learn enough from the episode to determine a possible underlying cause. Perhaps we will never know. Regardless, I do know that paying attention to all of Vinny's signs – body language, facial expressions, and eyes, will help me to understand him, care for him, and love him as best we can.

CITED STUDIES:

1. Wan M, Bolger N, Champagne FA. Human perception of fear in dogs varies according to experience with dogs. *PLoS ONE* 2012; 7:e51775. doi: 10.1371/journal.pone.0051775

2. Mariti C, Gazzano A, Moore JL, Baragli P, Chelli L, Sighieri C. Perception of dogs' stress by their owners. *Journal of Veterinary Behavior* 2012; 7:213-219.

27
Love Me, Love My Dog;
A New Twist on an Old Belief

Do people and their dogs share similar personality traits?

Everyone is familiar with that old saw about dogs looking like their owners. Certainly, there are plenty of photos of this genre floating around on Facebook pages and photo-sharing sites. However, look-alike dogs and owners aside, this common belief leads one to ask; Do dogs also *behave* similarly to their owners? Or more precisely, do dogs and their owners share personality traits? A group of collaborating scientists from Eotvos University's Family Dog Project in Hungary and from the Clever Dog Lab in Vienna, Austria asked exactly this question (1).

Background Information: Studies of human relationships provide quite a bit of scientific support for a theory called the *similarity-attraction hypothesis*. Rather than the "opposites attract" theory that prevails on TV sit-coms and in romance novels, it seems that friends and romantic partners who share personality traits, communication patterns, and yes, even degree of attractiveness have reduced conflict and disagreements and are generally happier in their relationships than are folks who tend to be more dissimilar from each other. Although not completely understood, it is presumed that hanging out with someone who mirrors our own values and self-perceptions supports our world view and enhances our feelings of security. (Hmmm.....so it really IS "*all about me*" in relationships, after all......). Which lead our researchers to ask, "*Given that many people have strong and enduring relationships with their dogs, does the similarity-attraction hypothesis operate when we choose our canine friends?*"

154

The Study: The investigators studied a group of 389 owner and dog pairs who had lived together for at least 10 months. Pairs were approximately evenly distributed between the Clever Dog Lab (Austria) and the Family Dog Project (Hungary). Owners completed a personality questionnaire about themselves that was designed to measure the "Big Five" personality traits of neuroticism, extraversion, conscientiousness, agreeableness, and openness. They also completed a modified Big Five questionnaire to describe their *dog's* personality, a measuring tool that had been previously validated in dogs by another group of researchers (2). Last, both the owner' and their dog's personalities were assessed independently by a peer and by a family member.

Results: The researchers examined factors that could influence owners' responses, such as the dogs' perceived versus actual personality traits, the number and age of dogs living in the home, and cultural differences between owners living in Austria and those living in Hungary. Overall, statistically significant correlations were found between the personalities of owners and the personality traits of their dogs, both when self-reported by the owners and as reported independently by another person. Here are a few specific results that may be of interest to other dog owners:

- **Anxious owners/anxious dogs:** While all five personality traits had significant correlations between owner and dog, the strongest association was found for neuroticism (ease of becoming upset, degree of emotional stability). In other words, anxious owners tended to live with anxious dogs (and vice versa; easy going owners like to hang out with tranquil dogs). The authors suggest that owners who are by nature more anxious may cause their dogs to become more nervous by behaving inconsistently, by being overly protective, or by failing to socialize their dogs adequately. Alternatively, the relationship may work in the opposite direction; a dog who is by nature more nervous may cause the owner to be distressed and anxious about the dog's behavior. (It is important

155

to remember that correlations do not imply causation - these results cannot provide evidence of the direction of these associations or even if there is a causative relationship).

- **It's not projection:** The study's results also showed that, contrary to popular belief (usually of non-dog folks), the similarities between owner and dog personalities were not the result of simple projection of the owner's self-perception onto his or her dog (for example, "*I think of myself as an open and outgoing extrovert; therefore, my dog is also the life of the party!*"). Both family member and peer ratings supported the significant correlations that were found between owner and dog personality traits.

- **Single versus multiple-dog homes:** Perhaps one of the most interesting results of this study had to do with comparisons between single and multiple dog homes and the order in which dogs were acquired. When an owner lived with two or more dogs, the similarity patterns between owners and the dogs differed, but tended to complement one another. For example, one dog might share a similar extraversion score with his owner, while the second dog's openness score positively correlated with her owner's score. The researchers speculated that these differences may reflect specific roles that each dog plays in the home, different reasons for obtaining the second or third dog, or even acquired differences as the dogs each develop their place in the family structure.

Take Away for Dog Folks: This study suggests that owners may often share one or more personality traits with their dogs, and that such observations reflect actual similarities rather than wishful thinking or the manifestation of popular folklore. The study could not tell us however, how these similarities come about. The most obvious explanation is that people consciously or subconsciously select a breed or an individual dog who matches their own personality in one or more ways. (Indeed, there is some evidence in the literature to support this). Alternatively, a dog's personality may converge with the traits of his owner over time as owner and dog learn from each other and develop a compatible lifestyle. However, the data from this study found no correlation between the length of ownership and degree of personality similarities, which suggests that this was not the case.

Regardless of the underlying cause, trainers, behaviorists and other dog professionals who work with dog-owner pairs can use this information as we encourage clients to recognize and capitalize upon all of the positive traits in their dogs. Emphasizing those traits that the owner and the dog share is likely to lead to appreciation rather than disdain, seeing that we humans have a tendency to recognize many of our own personality traits in a favorable light.

For me personally, this study certainly brings new meaning to the phrase "*Love me, Love my dog*". So, if you profess to care about me, then caring about my dogs should come quite easily for you as well, since chances are, we are a lot alike!

CITED STUDIES:

1. Turesdan B, Range F, Viranyi Z, et al. Birds of a feather flock together? Perceived personality matching in owner-dog dyads. *Applied Animal Behaviour Science* 2012; 140:154-160.

2. Gosling SD, Kwan VSY, John OP, et al. A dog's got personality: A cross-species comparative approach to personality judgments in dogs and humans. *Journal of Perspectives in Social Psychology* 2003; 85:1161-1169.

28
And Your Little Dog Too....

Do small dogs deserve their reputations?

Little dogs often get a bad rap. People who dislike small dogs say that they are yappy, hyper-excitable, nippy (reactive), untrained, and often spoiled (whatever that means). Indeed, it appears that even the Wicked Witch of the West had it in for the wee ones. So, are any of these beliefs true? Are little dogs truly as bratty as some would have us believe? If small dogs are found to exhibit more than their share of bad behaviors, are these inherent traits that come along with the miniaturized body type or does the owner shoulder some of the responsibility for junior's transgressions? Once again, we turn to science for some answers.

Background Information: When surveyed, owners of small and toy breed dogs have been found to rate their dogs as more excitable, disobedient, impulsive, and in some cases, more likely to bite, when compared with owners of large dogs (1-4). Factors that may contribute to reported differences between small and large dogs could originate with the dog, with the owner, or via idiosyncrasies of the relationship between the two. In 2010, a group of researchers at the Austrian University of Veterinary Medicine decided to study these factors to attempt to tease out an answer (5).

The Study: This was a large study. The authors surveyed almost 1300 dog owners in urban and suburban areas who were living with one or more companion dogs. The questionnaire collected information about owner and dog demographics, history of ownership, daily activities, dog care/training practices, and owner perceptions of their dog's behavior and response to commands. For this study, dogs were classified as "small" if they were reported to weigh less than 20 kg (~44 lb.) and large if they weighed 20 kg or more. Following collection of the completed surveys, the researchers used a statistical technique called Principle Component Analysis (PCA) to identify correlated groups of questions that suggest common underlying factors or themes. Three dog trait factors were identified: *Obedience, Aggression/excitability*, and *Anxiety/fearfulness*. Two primary owner factors that were found were *Consistency* and *Training Methods*, and the most important owner/dog relationship factor was *Shared Activities*.

Results: When the small and large groups of dogs were compared, several statistically significant (and interesting) differences were found:

- **The dogs:** Small dogs were reported by their owners to be significantly less obedient and significantly more excitable, anxious/fearful, and aggressive than were large dogs. These results confirm those reported by other researchers. However, contrary to many popular stereotypes about little dogs, it appears that the owners (not the dogs) were an important influencing factor in the expression of these undesirable behaviors.

- **The owners:** The owners of the small dogs were found to be less likely to train their dogs, less likely to play with their dogs, and were also less consistent during interactions with their dogs when compared with owners of large dogs. Moreover, significant positive correlations were found between frequency of play and interaction, owner consistency, and better obedience in the small dogs. While not evidence of causation, these correlations again suggest that it is the owners who have more to do with the reputation of little dogs than the dogs themselves.

- **Training methods:** This was the first study to compare the types of training methods used by owners of small and large dogs. No glaring differences were found, but small dog owners were found to use punishment (+P) less frequently than large dog owners. However, one should NOT use this result as evidence that "*small dogs need to be punished more frequently*", because the study also found that the frequent use of punishment during training was strongly correlated with an increase in aggressive behavior and excitability in *both* small and large dogs. Interestingly, greater reliance upon punishment during training was also associated with greater anxiety/fear in the small dogs, but not in the large dogs.

Study Strengths: Two definite strengths of this study were the number of dog owners that were interviewed and the detailed information that was collected. The large number of questions in the survey allowed the use of a statistical method (PCA) that identifies emerging concepts and that can enhance the reliability of results.

Study Limitations: Limitations are those observed for all volunteer survey studies. A self-selection bias is expected to occur, since people who are more interested in dog-related topics and therefore probably more committed to their dogs are more likely to respond. Second, results reflect owner perceptions rather than objectively measured behavior. Although owner bias must be considered, it is also true that owners know their dog best and that a researcher would be able to obtain only a short snapshot of each dog's behavior and habits. Direct observation by researchers would also indisputably reduce the number of owner/dog pairs that could be included in a study of this type - consider the logistics of attempting to interview and observe almost 1300 owner/dog pairs!

A final note regards the size categories that were used in this study. Dividing the dogs into two groups of less than 40 lbs. (small dogs) and greater than 40 lbs. (large dogs), may have missed some of the idiosyncratic dog and owner characteristics that are commonly reported in toy breed dogs, those of the 10 lbs. or less variety. Personally, I would have found it interesting if results for toy breed dogs, those that conveniently fit on laps and who are often carried rather than walked, had been reported and compared with larger dogs.

Take Away for Dog Folks: This study confirms what many people already suspect - that small dogs are not inherently little jerks, but rather it is their owners' inclination to tolerate undesirable behaviors and disinclination to spend time training and exercising their dogs that have led to Toto's nefarious reputation. As with certain other aspects of life, size does not matter. Little dogs, just like their big-boned cousins, require regular training and consistency and they thrive on daily exercise and play. And as this research shows, small dogs are less likely to become fearful, anxious, or show aggression when trained using methods that emphasize positive reinforcement than when trained using methods that emphasize punishment.

CITED STUDIES:

1. Bennett PC, Rohlf VI, Owner-companion dog interactions: Relationship between demographic variables, potentially problematic behaviours, training engagement and shared activities. *Applied Animal Behaviour Science* 2007; 102:65-84.

2. Guy NC, Luescher US, Dohoo SE, et al. A case series of biting dogs: characteristics of the dogs, their behaviour, and their victims. *Applied Animal Behaviour Science* 2001;74:43-57.

3. Kobelt AJ, Hemsworth PH, Barnett JL, ColemanCG. A survey of dog ownership in suburban Australia - conditions and behaviour problems. *Applied Animal Behaviour Science* 2003; 82:137-148.

4. Vas J, Topal J, Pech E, Miklosi A. measuring attention deficit and activity in dogs: A new application and validation of a human ADHD questionnaire. *Applied Animal Behaviour Science* 2007; 103:105-117.

5. Arhant C, Bubna-Littitz H, Bartels A, Futschik A, Troxler J. Be-
    haviour of small and larger dogs; Effects of training methods,
    inconsistency of owner behavior and level of engagement in
    activities with the dog. *Applied Animal Behaviour Science*
    2010; 123:131-142.

29
The Kids are Alright

A new look at dog bite prevention programs and the audiences that they are intended to educate.

According to the CDC, approximately 4.5 million people are bitten by dogs each year. Of these reported bites, a large victim demographic is children under the age of 10. Children are most likely to be bitten severely enough to require medical care or hospitalization. They are also most frequently bitten by their own dog or by a dog who they know, such as the dog belonging to a neighbor or relative. Bites to the face and neck are common in children, most likely because of their size and the types of behavior that they engage in with dogs.

Bite Prevention Programs for Kids: These alarming dog bite statistics have led to the development of bite prevention programs in many communities. Though few of these have been thoroughly studied or validated through research, there is some evidence showing these programs can positively influence the beliefs and behavior of children:

- **Prevent-A-Bite:** Grade school children (7 to 8 years of age) completed a 30-minute lesson that provided instruction for behaving appropriately and safely around dogs (1). Following the lesson, the children had the opportunity to interact with a friendly dog. Of the children who completed the program, only 9 percent behaved inappropriately with the dog. By comparison, 79 percent of children of the same age who had not completed the Prevent-A-Bite lesson (the control group) showed inappropriate behavior upon meeting the dog.

- **BARK Program (Be Aware, Responsible and Kind):** This study was a pre-test/post-test evaluation with 500 children, aged 6 to 9 years (2). After reading and completing activity workbooks and watching a video, children showed improved knowledge about how to behave with dogs. (Note: This study did not include a test with a live dog).

- **Delta DogSafe Program:** A group of young children, 3 to 5 years of age, completed a program that used photographs and a puppet show to model safe behavior with dogs (3). Children who completed the training were more likely to recognize potentially dangerous behaviors depicted in dogs in photographs than children who had not completed the training. (Note: This study did not include a test with a live dog).

- **The Blue Dog Program:** *The Blue Dog* is an interactive computer program designed for children between 3 and 6 years of age and their parents. It includes a series of animated scenarios of a dog and a child and the user must make decisions about how (or if) the child character interacts with the dog in each scene. The program provides instant feedback regarding appropriate behavior with dogs. A recent study examined the learning outcomes of using *Blue Dog* in 76 children (4). After a week of using the program with their parents, children were better able to recognize risky situations when shown photographs of dogs. However, the children who had used the program did not change their actual behavior when presented with an unfamiliar live dog or when tested using scenarios with dolls.

The *Kids* are Alright: The results of these studies suggest that children can benefit from dog bite prevention programs in terms of their reported knowledge, and that older children can transfer these lessons to live interactions with unfamiliar dogs. It appears that the transfer of understanding into behavior may be less effective in younger children, however. (Note: No studies to date

164

have evaluated post-test behaviors with familiar dogs, an important issue seeing that the majority of bites come from known dogs).

The *Parents*, on the Other Hand: In their 2011 study of Blue Dog, David Schwebel, Barbara Morrongiello and their colleagues also collected data from the parents of the 3- to 6-year-olds. They reported some rather disturbing findings:

- *76 percent* of the parents believed that their child already knew most or all of the information that Blue Dog provided (remember, these kids were just 3 to 6 years of age).

- A majority of parents (65 %) also believed that their child would apply most or all of what they learned from the program to interactions with their own dog. (Seems to be rather contradictory, seeing that they believed their kid already knew everything.......I was confused).

- And, most parents admitted that they did *not* read the Parent Guide completely (93 percent actually), which included information about safe behavior between children and dogs. (It appears that the parents were certain that they too already knew everything there was to know about proper dog interactions).

Given that parental supervision and good judgment are key components to safe interactions between small children and dogs, the same group of researchers decided to test the effectiveness of *Blue Dog* training on the behavior of *parents* - specifically how parental supervision during interactions between children and dogs was influenced by completion of *Blue Dog* training (5).

The Study: The researchers had two objectives. First, they examined the typical supervisory practices of parents of preschool children when their child was in the presence of an unfamiliar dog. They then assessed changes in parental supervision several weeks after the parents had completed the *Blue Dog* program with their child. The study groups included 55 child/parent pairs, each of which lived with at least one adult dog. Half of the families completed *Blue Dog* training and half (the control group) completed a similar type of computer program that provided fire safety education. A pre/post-test method was used in which the parent and the child were brought into a room in which a gentle and friendly dog was present with his/her trainer. The parents were given no information about the dog's temperament and were told that there would be a dog in the room immediately prior to entering the room. Measured parent outcomes included reactions to seeing their child in the vicinity of an unfamiliar dog and to interacting with the dog and their use of supervisory behaviors.

Results: Results were reported for the pre-test (before *Blue Dog* training) and post-test (after *Blue Dog* Training) sessions.

- **Pre-test session:** Children in both the test group and the control group showed cautious behaviors upon seeing the unfamiliar dog. In contrast, the majority of the parents demonstrated risky behaviors that included encouraging their child to immediately approach the dog or immediately approaching the dog themselves. Most of the children did eventually interact with the dog, either on their own or as a result of encouragement from the parent. There were no differences between the test group and the control group, but.....*here's the kicker......the collective behaviors of the parents were scored as being significantly more risky than those of their children.*

- **Post-test session:** Following *Blue Dog* training, once again, the children were appropriately cautious when confronted with an unfamiliar dog (a different dog from session 1). Their parents, on the other hand, continued to demonstrate risky behaviors. (Parental behavior trended toward less risky behaviors after the training, but the difference was not statistically significant; $p = 0.07$ [Note; $p < 0.05$ is generally considered to be statistically significant]). Following training, there were no significant differences between the test group that had completed *Blue Dog* and the control group - in other words, the training had no statistically significant effect on the behavior of either the children or their parents. (The children continued to behave cautiously; the parents, well, they continued to behave badly).

- **Both sessions:** In both sessions, parents stayed in proximity of their children and demonstrated high degrees of attentiveness. This result is an important one because it showed that while the parents' behaviors with the dog and with the child-dog interactions were unsafe, they consistently demonstrated an overall level of good general parenting supervision.

The results of this study suggest that a large proportion of the problem, at least for young children, lies not with the kids, but with *their parents*. The problem appears to NOT be one of inattention or poor supervision, as the parents in this study did stay in close proximity to their children and did pay attention to them. Rather, at issue is parents' beliefs about appropriate behaviors when interacting (and encouraging their child to interact) with dogs.

Up on my Soapbox

Draggin' Out the Ol' Soap Box Again: Like many dog trainers, I cringe when new clients say to me "*Oh, our Rover is such a great dog! My kids and their friends can do anything to him - sit on him, grab his skin, pull his tail, and he just takes it! Isn't he a wonderful family dog?*". Similarly, my teeth clench when I open emails from well-meaning (though misguided) people who send me outrageous photos of their small child and dog because "*You like dogs, so you will love this photo of little Johnny crawling on top of our dog*". Yeah.....well, no.

To All Parents: Your child should not sit on your dog while reading a book. Nor should he ride your dog like a pony, sprawl across her whilst she is napping, grab your dog's face in his fist, pull on her skin or tail, or stick a hand into her food bowl. Not only are these behaviors disrespectful and borderline (sometimes not even borderline) abusive, but they are dangerous. Your loving, sweet family dog who has finally had enough abuse and air snaps at your child in response to these unsafe behaviors will pay dearly for that snap if she makes contact. Both your child and your dog pay (with the dog possibly paying the ultimate price - her life). All for a photo op and some increased Facebook traffic? Not only should you prevent your child from doing these things (even if you live with that wonderful dog who allows it), you should model kindness and respect and proper interactions with dogs - all dogs - starting with your own.

CITED STUDIES:

1. Chapman S, Cornwall J, Righetti, Sung J. Preventing dog bites in children: randomized controlled trial of an educational intervention. British Medical Journal 2000; 320:1512-1513.

2. Spiegel IB. A pilot study to evaluate an elementary school-based dog bite prevention program. *Anthrozoos* 2000; 13:164-173.

3. Wilson F, Dwyer F, Bennett PC. Prevention of dog bites: Evaluation of a brief educational intervention program for children. *Journal of Community Psychology* 2003; 31:75-86.

4. Schwebel DC, Morrongiello BA, Davis AL, et al. *The Blue Dog*: Evaluation of an interactive software program to teach young children how to interact safely with dogs. *Journal of Pediatric Psychology* 2012; 37:272-281.

5. Morrongiello BA, Schwebel DC, Stewart J, et al. Examining parents' behaviors and supervision of their children in the presence of an unfamiliar dog: Does *The Blue Dog* intervention improve parent practices? *Accident Analysis and Prevention* 2013; 54:108-113.

30
Dog Park People

*A study examines the behavior of dogs and their people
at a community dog park. What it reports is not pretty.*

Dog Parks are a relatively new cultural phenomenon, and have
been increasing in both number and popularity over the last 15
years. Although almost every community has one, it is an under-
statement to say that people are rather polarized in their views
of dog parks. Advocates maintain that these designated areas
provide invaluable opportunities for dogs to enjoy off-lead exercise, socialization and play with other dogs, and for owners to
meet and befriend like-minded people in their communities. At
the other end of the spectrum, critics argue that off-lead dog areas are often poorly managed and supervised and present unac-
ceptable risks to dogs. These risks include aggressive (or preda-
tory) attacks, physical injuries caused by large groups of dogs
running together, and the transmission of parasites and disease.

Dog Park People: A study that was published in 2012 focused
not on the dogs who visit dog parks, but rather upon the *people*
who give them the ride there - their owners (1). Patrick Jackson,
a sociologist at Sonoma State University in California, was interested in the emerging social norms and group dynamics of people who gathered regularly at a community dog park with their
dogs.

The Study: The author used an *ethnographic method* of data collection, an approach that is commonly used by sociologists when
studying complex interactions among people. Over a period of
15 months, Jackson visited a local community dog park with his
two dogs. They visited the park between three and five times per
week and at various times during the day. He collected data that

included owner and dog demographics, activity patterns and spatial distributions of people and dogs, visit durations, topics of conversation among owners, frequency and type of conflicts between dogs, and approaches used by owners to resolve problems. Data were recorded during visits and immediately afterward and behaviors and interactions were coded according to emergent themes and patterns.

Results: A number of owner behaviors and interaction types were found to be consistent from day-to-day and appeared to represent the social norms of the dog park that was studied:

- **Public demonstration of owner-dog connection:** Dog park visitors frequently (and often repeatedly during a visit) demonstrated their attachment to their dog through active play with the dog, offering (and often receiving in return) friendly eye contact, and speaking to (and for) their dog. This public display of connection appears to be an important component of dog park culture as it allows all visitors to place each dog with his/her owner.

- **Types of problems:** Four major types of dog problems were regularly observed. These included: mobbing/aggression at the gated entry into the park; mounting behaviors; aggressive behavior (attacks and fights); and feces clean-up issues. Behavior problems that dogs showed that were considered annoying but not necessarily in need of intervention included jumping on people, urinating on the benches, and excessive attention-seeking behaviors toward people other than the owner.

- **Owner responses to problems:** Jackson identified a set of approaches that the park attendees regularly used to avoid or respond to problems in the park. These were summarized as:

Avoidance: This occurred when people witnessed a commotion such as a dog fight or a dog being mobbed by several dogs at the gate. Others in the park would simply *"steer clear"* of the area and would not get involved.

Leaving the area or the park: This tactic was observed both by people whose dogs had been attacked or were being repeatedly mounted by another dog (see below) as well as by owners whose dogs were the misbehaving party. Owners of dogs who had been attacked or bullied typically left angry and upset. Owners of dogs who had misbehaved often moved to another area of the park or "left early".

Humor and baby talk: Humor was reported to occur most frequently when one dog was mounting another. Sex jokes were apparently popular (really?). Humor was also used at the expense of owners whose dogs were being mounted by another dog (and were trying to stop it) or were upset about the behavior of other dogs or owners. Finally, some owners would use remedial (baby) talk to their dogs to ostensibly chastise them for their bouts of misbehavior while doing nothing to actually stop or prevent the behavior or to help the targeted victim.

Disturbing Stories: As I read and then reread this paper, it was impossible to ignore its complete exclusion of any mention whatsoever of the potential or actual harm that came to many of the dogs whose stories were being told. Many were situations in which a dog was being emotionally harmed and possibly physically injured. Here are four examples that the author reports:

- Immediately after entering the park, a dog stares down and then chases another dog, holding his head over the retreating dog's shoulder and snarling. The dog then switches to another dog, continuing this behavior. (*Owner: Does nothing. Other owners: Watch and say/do nothing*).

- A black Labrador mounts another dog and will not stop. The targeted dog's owner repeatedly attempts to get the Lab off of her dog, to no avail. Four people standing nearby watch this and laugh. The dog's owner finally succeeds in removing the Lab from her dog. Upset and angry, she leaves the park. The observing owners joke about the incident.

- An older dog is attacked by a young dog. The fight is prolonged and the owners have difficulty breaking the two dogs apart. Following the attack, the young dog's owner said to his dog: "*Bad dog; lie down, sit down. We are going home early because of you.*"

- A dog's ear was bitten off (yes, her EAR) by another dog. The author states that this problem was "resolved" because the attacking dog's owner offered to pay the veterinary bill. This incident is reported in a section describing ways in which owners "over-react" to problems.

Up on my Soapbox

Soapbox Time: I should admit at the forefront that I am personally not a fan of dog parks. My reasons include all of those mentioned at the start of this essay plus the fact that I genuinely just prefer to go walking or running alone with my dogs. However, a small but significant number of my training school students frequent dog parks because they provide an opportunity for off-lead exercise and play with other dogs. While it is not for me, I have always respected their choice and have provided students

173

with the usual set of precautions that have hopefully kept their dogs safe.

Until now. I honestly began writing this essay with every intention of focusing on the topic of the study - the behavior and social interactions of people who visit a dog park with their dogs. And, admittedly, the paper does present some interesting themes and observations about emerging social norms of the dog park. However, rather than provide needed research about developing cultural norms of dog parks, this study ultimately provides evidence that: (1) Dog parks are not safe for dogs; and (2) Dog park people frequently behave badly by not being responsible dog owners and by being inconsiderate and uncaring towards other people and their dogs.

Granted, this ethnographic study examined the cultural milieu of a single dog park. Certainly dog parks vary in size, type of rules, participant behavior, and numerous other factors. And of course, more research is needed. However, until a study comes along that convinces me otherwise, I will continue to hike and run with my dogs for exercise and companionship, and to provide play times for them with doggie friends who they know well (and whose owners I know and trust as responsible and caring dog people). I am also going to modify my advice to my training school clients. For those who tell us that they visit dog parks, I will encourage them to instead seek less risky (and more dog- *and* people-friendly) ways to exercise and socialize their dogs. And, for those who continue to visit dog parks, I will advise that they be cautious not only regarding the behavior of other dogs at the park, but regarding the other owners as well.

CITED STUDY:

Jackson P. Situated activities in a dog park: Identity and conflict in human-animal space. *Society and Animals* 2012; 20:254-272.

31
Lend a Helping Paw

A new study examines whether dogs are naturally motivated to help others – their results may surprise you.

Dogs are highly social beings who express their social nature in a variety of ways. They desire companionship with others and readily integrate into our human families and lives. Most of our dogs love to play and to learn new things and enjoy spending time together going for walks, a ride in the car or simply hanging out for a cuddle on the couch. Given the choice, most dogs prefer to share their days with their human family rather than alone and many also have strong social relationships (friendships) with other dogs or even with members of other species.

Prosocial Behavior: Although not yet studied thoroughly, dogs may also exhibit certain types of "prosocial" behavior. These are spontaneous actions that are intended to help another individual in some way, usually with no obvious benefit to the helper. Psychologists have defined four general categories of prosocial behavior. These are comforting, sharing, informing and helping. At least anecdotally, comforting is something that dogs seem to excel at. Many dog owners relate that their dog is very empathic, seems to know when they are sad or are having a bad day, and often stays close at hand to provide comfort and love. Behaviors related to sharing may be less common, but certainly many of us have known a dog or two who readily shares his toys, bed or food with others.

What about the most complex prosocial behavior - Helping? There is no doubt that dogs can be successfully *trained* to help humans. Examples abound and include dogs who aid the disabled, move or protect livestock, find illicit contraband, and perform in search and rescue operations. The number and variety of

175

trained skills that dogs use to help us are both vast and impressive. However, *prosocial helping* is a bit different because this type of aid occurs spontaneously with little or no former training. Prosocial helping behavior is intrinsically (internally) motivated by empathy or a sense of community and occurs without an obvious or anticipated reward to the performer.

For dogs, this form of helping is considered to be a relatively complex social behavior because it requires two things. First, the dog must understand the goal of the person who is in need. Second, the dog must be motivated to help the person to achieve that goal. For example, in the case of helping a person to find something, the dog has to understand that something is hidden/lost and that the owner is searching for it (and wants it) and must also have a desire (i.e. be motivated) to help the person to find the object. It is this second component of helping, the intrinsic or internal motivation to help others, that a group of researchers at the Max Planck Institute for Evolutionary Anthropology in Germany recently studied. They asked the question: *"Are dogs inclined to lend a helping paw?"*

The Study: The researchers conducted a series of four experiments to determine whether dogs would come to the aid of a person who was attempting to enter another room to retrieve a set of keys. The same scenario was used in each of the four experiments, but the identity of the person and the way in which the person communicated his goal to the dog were varied. The dogs were first trained to open a Plexiglas door that entered into a small room (i.e. the target room) by hitting a button that was positioned on the ground in front of the door. The dogs were trained using shaping and positive reinforcement (food treats). The training took place several days prior to the actual experiment and only dogs who successfully learned to hit the button were included in the experiment. The behavior used for opening the door was purposely trained *without* a cue, to ensure that the dogs learned how to open the door but were not trained to respond to a specific command to do so.

176

Experimental Conditions: During each experiment, a research-er or the dog's owner communicated to the dog their desire to enter the target room by one of several means. These included either pushing on the door, reaching for the door, pointing at the button, using gaze (either into the room alone or alternating be-tween the room and the dog), talking (general terms), command-ing the dog, or a combination of spontaneous (natural) commu-nicative gestures. In all conditions, the goal that the owner or experimenter was attempting to communicate to the dog was that they needed to enter the target room to retrieve the keys that were on the floor. Both the dogs and the person could easily see into the target room (Note: Keys were purposely used as an object that would have no or little value to the dogs, thus ensur-ing that their inclination to help was not motivated by a desire to retrieve a toy or to obtain food). In each experiment, the control was a person who sat near the dog but did not communicate a desire to enter the target room.

Results: Dogs were highly likely to help in two primary condi-tions. These were either when the person used pointing gestures that were directed toward the button that opened the door or when the person used a variety of "natural" communication ges-tures simultaneously such as gesturing, talking, gazing and pointing to express their goal. Interestingly, the person's identity did not influence the dog's response. Dogs were as likely to help a stranger as they were to help their owner. The researchers concluded that the dogs in this study were highly motivated to help a human when the person's goal was clearly communicated using either a common communication signal (pointing) or a va-riety of naturally selected gestures in combination. They sug-gested that an absence of helping behavior in dogs may be more likely occur when dogs do not understand the person's goal, ra-ther than due to the lack of an intrinsic desire to be of aid.

Researchers who study dog cognition are interested in whether dogs are capable of understanding human communicative ges-tures as being informative (i.e. providing helpful information)

177

rather than interpreting them only as imperative (i.e. as a command to do something). This is an important distinction because while it is well-known that dogs can be trained to perform quite complex tasks and respond to trained cues, there is not that much scientific evidence showing us that dogs regularly use human behavior as information (although anecdotal evidence of this certainly abounds). The results of this study, and a few others before it, suggest that dogs are capable of perceiving certain human gestures, such as pointing and gazing, as information and that they may subsequently use that information to act (and help).

Take Away for Dog Folks: The results of this study emphasize some important issues about how we communicate with dogs. When isolated gestures or verbal commands were used to attempt to communicate the person's goals, dogs did not perform well. Give this a try and see how unnatural it feels. Point or gaze at something near your dog but do not use any additional words, body language or gaze. Does your dog respond? (Mine did not - they just looked at me like I was a crazy person). Conversely, when owners were instructed to just "communicate naturally" with their dog using a myriad of signals, dogs' understanding and success improved dramatically. While this difference is not all that surprising, it is important information for trainers and owners to keep in mind. Simply issuing a command or gesturing stiffly won't cut the mustard with most dogs. Similar to communicating with the humans in our lives, effective communication with dogs includes a variety of simultaneously delivered verbal and non-verbal signals - signals that can be messy and complex and difficult to define, but ultimately that are most successful at getting the message across.

On a deeper level, this study informs us about empathy. We would all agree that dogs are of great help to us, in a myriad of ways. We train dogs to aid the disabled, protect us, find lost children, and comfort the ill. However, that type of helping (while noteworthy and admirable in its own right) differs qualitatively from spontaneous helping in which the dog perceives a need and, presumably motivated by empathy, reacts by providing aid. It is this latter form of helping that was tested in this study. The cleverly designed set of experiments showed that when the goal of the person was clearly communicated to the dogs, many immediately helped the experimenter - and did so even when there was no obvious reward available to them. While all dog lovers know in our heart of hearts that our dogs express love, concern, and even compassion for others, here is some science showing us that contrary to the beliefs of an ever declining few, humans do not have a corner on the empathy market. Once understanding is achieved, our dogs are willing to help us - even with something as mundane as helping someone to enter a room to retrieve some keys! (Just think about what they may be capable of when we really need their help). Have some fun - Test your own dog and find out if he is willing to lend you a helping paw!

CITED STUDY:

Brauer J, Schonefeld K, Call J. When do dogs help humans? *Applied Animal Behaviour Science* 2013; 148:138-149.

32
The Sniff(th) Sense

Starting with a mole-sniffing Border Collie Mix, what does the current evidence tell us about dogs' ability to detect cancer in people?

The dog's extraordinary olfactory abilities are put to a lot of use today. Dogs are trained to indicate the presence of contraband, find lost people, search natural disaster areas, and even find victims of drowning. We also train our dogs to use their noses in a wide range of dog sports such as tracking, obedience and canine nose-work. Another talent that dogs (at least some dogs) may possess and that is receiving increasing attention is the ability to detect the presence of disease in human patients. While the detection of several chronic health problems has been examined, including diabetes, seizure disorders and heart disease, the dog's ability to identify the presence of cancer in human patients as a diagnostic early screening approach is especially intriguing.

It All Started with a Mole-Sniffing Border Collie: Almost 25 years ago, a letter from two doctors was published in the scientific journal, *The Lancet*. The letter described the case of a 44-year-old woman whose Border Collie mix had started to fixate on a mole located on her leg. Over a period of several weeks, the dog repeatedly sniffed and licked the area, eventually escalating his behavior to biting at the spot. Concerned, the owner visited her doctor, only to discover that the mole had developed into a malignant melanoma. Over the next few years, an increasing number of similar cases were reported, all variations of the scenario in which a pet dog spontaneously alerted his or her owner to the presence of a cancerous tumor. These were not just mole fixations – dogs were reportedly finding a wide range of disease, including bladder, breast, lung, prostate, and ovarian cancers. As anecdotal evidence, these cases raised the question of whether dogs could be trained to reliably detect cancer and ultimately be used as screening aids for diagnosing malignancies at an early stage.

The Studies: A wide range of research studies has examined the use of dogs to detect cancer, which is remarkable given the relatively few years of interest in this area of study. However, while the total number of studies is high, they vary tremendously in significant factors such as type of cancer, the number, breed and age of dogs, training methods, and the type of samples used for detection. Cancers that have been studied include skin (melanoma), prostate, lung, breast, bladder, colorectal and breast. Dogs have also been trained to detect cancer using tumor cells, urine, blood, feces and exhaled breath. Although not always reported, *all* of the described training methods used positive reinforcement and several studies employed clicker training. However, training methods, intensity and duration have differed, as well as the experience level of the trainers involved.

What Have We Learned? Keeping these disparities in mind, have we learned anything of a general nature from these studies? First, the good news. *Dogs can do this* (at least under controlled, experimental conditions). For example, a Belgian Malinois selected from a group of dogs being trained for explosives detection work and professionally trained to differentiate between the urine of healthy men and the urine of men with prostate cancer successfully identified cancer in 31 of 33 cases (1). Another study also tested the ability of a professionally trained scent detection dog to identify the presence of colorectal cancer in stool and breath samples (2). When tested in 37 trials, the dog correctly identified cancer when it was present 91 percent of the time and missed a correct diagnosis just 1 percent of the time. In the largest of the published studies, four trained dogs were tested using 220 breath samples from patients suspected of having lung cancer (3). The dogs accurately identified lung cancer 71 percent of the time, although there was a great deal of variation among the four dogs in their ability to correctly detect cancer when it was present (called sensitivity). This variability may have occurred because the researchers used pet dogs for the study rather than dogs that were specifically selected for scent discrimination tasks, as were the dogs in the previous studies. Similar inconsistencies among dogs were reported when experimenters trained a group of six unselected (pet) dogs for detection of melanoma, breast or lung cancer (4). While most studies trained dogs to detect a single type of cancer, one group of researchers tested five dogs who were trained to detect either lung or breast cancer (5). They reported almost 100 percent accuracy when the dogs were tested with lung cancer patients and almost 90 percent accuracy when they were tested with breast cancer patients. Success at varying rates has also been reported in dogs trained to detect bladder cancer in urine samples, ovarian cancer in blood or tissue, and melanoma from skin tissue samples (6,7,8).

Proof of Principle vs. Use in Practice: Most of the currently available studies make the point that their results should be viewed primarily as "proof-of-principle" studies. In other words, these studies show us that yes, indeed, dogs have extraordinary scenting capabilities and also that some dogs can be successfully trained to reliably detect the presence of cancer in human tissues. Pretty cool stuff, indeed. Taken at this level, I think most would agree that the results of the current cancer detection studies provide additional evidence to the already multitudinous piles that the dog has a remarkable nose. Most dog people, myself included, are pretty darned impressed by these data.

However, the jump from knowing that dogs can do this amazing feat to using dogs as early screening detectors for cancer in human patients is one very big (and perhaps unattainable) jump. There are a number of obstacles that need to be cleared for such a role to become reliable, economical and accepted by medical professionals and patients. Perhaps most important is to first attain a better understanding of what exactly these dogs are doing.

What Are They Smelling? Cancer cells, along with some of the changes that occur in the body in response to cancer, produce a wide range of unique substances that emit very specific odors. As a group these are called volatile organic compounds (VOCs), which means that they contain carbon atoms and have airborne properties (i.e. they can be sniffed). Because the set of VOCs varies with the type of cancer, researchers refer to these collectively as a cancer's "odor signature". However, there are gaps in our knowledge about these compounds. First, not all of the biologically significant molecules that are produced by cancer cells have been identified, nor do researchers have well defined odor signatures for all forms and stages of cancer. Although each cancer is presumed to a unique set of VOCs, these may vary with stage of disease, location of the tumor, presence of other illnesses, and with the age, health or genetic make-up of the patient. Similarly, the type of sample that is used (urine, breath, tissue) is expected to affect which VOCs are present.

It is presumed, but not known, that dogs who can successfully differentiate between non-cancerous, healthy cells and cells or secretions that are cancerous are detecting the presence of that cancer's odor signature – its particular set of VOCs. It is also presumed that most of these odors exist at levels that are undetectable by the human nose but are present at levels that a dog's nose is capable of detecting. The problem lies in understanding exactly which compound or compounds in the overall signature that the dogs are learning to detect. From a practical stand-point, this means that dogs are being trained to detect a cancer odor signature that is still incompletely understood and to compounds that as of yet have not been identified. Therefore, if a dog who has completed training misdiagnoses a sample, it is impossible to trouble-shoot errors to determine the reason that the dog failed, since we do not know exactly what the dog is looking for or if the compound is consistently found in all patients, of all ages, and all stages of disease with that particular cancer.

Scent Memory? It is known that the dog has an astounding ability to form "scent memories". This means that dogs are capable of recognizing odors that they have encountered previously and that they have a high capacity to store memories of a large number of individual odors. A helpful analogy is to consider how many faces you recognize of people you have met during your lifetime. For most of us, this is a really large number, yet we readily recognize people who we may have only met a few times or have not seen in a long time. Research has shown that humans have an astounding ability to remember up to thousands of faces, even those that we have experienced only via photographs! Think of the dog's nose in the same way. While we excel at recognizing human faces, the dog excels at recognizing distinct odors. This is an important consideration given that we do not know exactly what it is that dogs are smelling when they detect cancer in an experiment.

This is of consequence because training dogs for scent detection work involves taking a set of known (target) odor samples that are repeatedly used to teach the dog to identify and indicate the target odor. For cancer detection training, these samples come from patients who are confirmed to have a particular type of cancer. A challenge lies in the fact that such samples are a limited resource, both in terms of the number that can be obtained from medical centers and in sample viability (i.e. how long they can be stored and retain their scent odor for reuse). On a practical level, this means that most dogs used in these studies have been trained using a relatively small set of cancer-containing samples. Once they are trained and are demonstrating proficiency on the known samples, the dogs are then tested on either planted samples (healthy patients with hidden cancer-samples on their body) or with actual patients. A challenge that researchers have faced is determining whether dogs are generalizing what they learn during training on a small set of samples to the general population of patients whose scent signatures will vary in unknown ways. At question is whether the dogs have learned to identify a general cancer odor signature or have simply memorized some components of the samples that they were trained with. If it is the latter, the dogs would be expected to fail when tested using a large population of patients who may or may not have a similar odor signature to the training set.

A recent study using dogs trained to detect prostate cancer attempted to tackle the issue of scent memory (9).The researchers clicker trained 10 dogs through three incremental stages of training to detect prostate cancer from urine samples. At the conclusion of the training, only two dogs demonstrated high proficiency in detecting cancer using the training samples. These dogs were then tested on a large set of unique samples (both cancer and controls). During the actual tests, neither of the dogs successfully indicated cancer samples from healthy samples at a frequency that was greater than that expected by chance. The researchers suggested that an explanation for this failure was that during training, the dogs had memorized the odors of each of the training samples and while they clearly were able to discriminate between those samples and healthy patient samples, they did not subsequently generalize that ability to the odor signature present in the urine of the large group of prostate cancer patients that was tested. It must also be mentioned that like some of the earlier studies that demonstrated low proficiency, the dogs in this study were selected from a group of pet dogs whose owners were attending a local dog training school rather than from dogs that were specifically selected and trained for scent work.

Patients with Other Illnesses: Most of the studies reported to date have tested dogs' accuracy at cancer detection against samples from healthy volunteers. However, many people who have cancer also have other health problems or benign disease. Because false positives cause extreme anxiety and can lead to unneeded biopsies or treatment, minimizing this type of error is of enormous importance when considering the reliability of early screening techniques. While it appears that (some) dogs are capable of consistently discriminating between healthy and cancerous patients, can they make this distinction when faced with people who may have complicating disease?

Only two studies have tested this ability. The large lung cancer study discussed previously also tested the ability of their four trained dogs to differentiate between patients with confirmed lung cancer and patients afflicted with another (non-cancerous) lung disease, chronic obstructive pulmonary disease (COPD) (3). They found that while the dogs were still capable of identifying patients who had lung cancer, their success rate decreased somewhat then they had to distinguish between cancer and COPD. A more recent study, published in early 2014, was less promising (10). A group of four trained dogs were found to be highly effective when distinguishing between patients who were healthy (had no lung disease) and patients who had some type of lung disease. However, when tested to determine if they could distinguish between benign and cancerous lung tumors, the dogs' accuracy decreased dramatically. For example, the dogs performed with 99 percent sensitivity in the initial tests of healthy versus not heathy patients, but this decreased to 56 t0 76 percent (depending on the dog), when they were required to discriminate between malignant and benign lung conditions. In terms of false positives – this means that up to 44 percent of the cases were identified as cancerous when they were not – not a good result for a screening tool for cancer.

Take Away for Dog Folks; We're Not There Yet: As dog lovers, we all would like to see cancer detection as one more way in which our beloved dogs show themselves to be capable of helping us. We all want to believe that dogs can be trained to reliably predict the presence of cancerous cells in a human patient and that once we have the training properly nailed down, these dogs will show themselves to be superior to other screening tests that may be invasive in nature, costly, or not sensitive enough to catch cancer in its early stages. At this point in the dog sniffing game, it appears that some dogs are able to detect some cancers, some of the time, and that this detection is most successful when dogs are carefully selected for scent training work and when they are asked to compare potential cancer patients with healthy patients. Challenges lie ahead in determining what exactly it is that dogs are sniffing, refining and standardizing training, increasing accuracy and reliability, and completing more rigorous, double-blind, well-controlled studies. Regardless, in my view, because these studies do provide "proof of principle" they give us one more reason to be in awe of and thankful for our canine friends and their amazing sniff(th) sense!

CITED STUDIES:

1. Cornu JN, Cancel-Tassin G, Ondet V, Giradet C, Cussernot O. Olfactory detection of prostate cancer by dogs sniffing urine: A step forward in early diagnosis. *European Urology* 2011; 59:197-201.

2. Sonoda H, Kohnoe S, Yamazato T. Colorectal cancer screening with odour material by canine scent detection. *Gut* 2011; 60:814-819.

3. Ehmann R, Boedeker E, Friedrich U, Sagert J, Dippon J, Friedel G, Walles T. Canine scent detection in the diagnosis of lung cancer: Revisiting a puzzling phenomenon. *European Respiration Journal* 2012; 39:669-676.

4. Walczak M, Jezierski T, Gorecka-Bruzda A, Sobczynska M, Ensminger J. Impact of individual training parameters and manner of taking breath odor samples on the reliability of canines as cancer screeners. *Journal of Veterinary Behavior* 2012; 7:283-294.

5. McCulloch M, Jezierski T, Broffman M, Hubbard A, Turner K, Janecki T. Diagnostic accuracy of canine scent detection in early- and late-stage lung and breast cancers. *Integrative Cancer Therapies* 2006; 5:30-39.

6. Willis CM, Church SM, Guest CM. Olfactory detection of human bladder cancer by dogs: proof of principle study. *British Medical Journal* 2004; 329:712.

7. Pickel D, Manucy GP, Walker DB, Hall SB, Walker JC. Evidence for canine olfactory detection of melanoma. *Applied Animal Behaviour Science* 2004: 89:107-116.

8. Horvath G, Andersson H, Paulsson G. Characteristic odour in the blood reveals ovarian carcinoma. *BMC Cancer* 2010; 10:643-646.

9. Elliker KR, Sommervillw BA, Broom DM, Neal DE, Armstrong S, Williams HC. Key considerations for the experimental training and evaluation of cancer odour detection dogs: Lessons learnt from a double-blind, controlled trial of prostate cancer detection. *BMC Urology* 2014;14:22-31.

10. Amundsen T, Sundstrom S, Buvik T, Gederaas OA, Haaverstad R. Can dogs smell lung cancer? First study using exhaled breath and urine screening in unselected patients with suspected lung cancer. *Acta Oncologica* 2014;53:307-315.

About the Author

Linda Case is a canine nutritionist, dog trainer, and science writer. She earned her B.S. in Animal Science at Cornell University and her M.S. in Canine/Feline Nutrition at the University of Illinois. Following graduate school, Linda was a lecturer in canine and feline science in the Animal Sciences Department at the University of Illinois for 15 years and then taught companion animal behavior and training at the College of Veterinary Medicine.

Linda owns AutumnGold Consulting and Dog Training Center in Mahomet, IL (www.autumngoldconsulting.com), a company that provides scientific writing and training programs to dog owners, pet food companies and animal advocacy organizations. Linda is the author of numerous publications and six other books, including most recently, *Dog Food Logic: Making Smart Decisions for your Dog in an Age of Too Many Choices* (Dogwise, 2014). She also authors the popular blog "The Science Dog" which regularly reviews new research in canine behavior, training, nutrition and health and where many of the essays in "Beware the Straw Mam" originated (http://thesciencedog.wordpress.com).

Linda and her husband Mike share their lives with four dogs; Cadie, Vinny, Chip, and Cooper, and Pete the cat. In addition to dog training, Linda enjoys running, hiking, swimming, and gardening—activities that she happily shares with all of her dogs.

Contact information:
Linda P. Case, MS
Owner, AutumnGold Consulting and Dog Training Center
www.autumngoldconsulting.com

Made in the USA
San Bernardino, CA
06 January 2015